Lift As You Climb

www.penguin.co.uk

LIFT AS YOU CLIMB

Women, Ambition
and How to Change the Story

VIV GROSKOP

Printed in the USA 1307 Avenue Road LTPB by Above (UK), Milton and
Printed and bound in Italy by Grafica Veneta S.p.A.

Authorised representative in the EEA is Penguin Random House
Morrison Chambers, 32 Nassau Street, Dublin D02 YH68

Penguin Random House is committed to a sustainable
future for our business and our planet. This book
is made from Forest Stewardship Council® certified paper

BLACK SWAN

TRANSWORLD PUBLISHERS
Penguin Random House, One Embassy Gardens,
8 Viaduct Gardens, London SW11 7BW
www.penguin.co.uk

Transworld is part of the Penguin Random House group of companies
whose addresses can be found at global.penguinrandomhouse.com

First published in Great Britain in 2020 by Bantam Press
an imprint of Transworld Publishers
Black Swan edition published 2021

A CIP catalogue record for this book is available from the British Library.

ISBN
9781784166113

Typeset in 10.25/15pt Arno by Novel IT Bradstock, Milton Keynes.
Printed and bound in Italy by Grafica Veneta S.p.A.

The authorised representative in the EEA is Penguin Random House Ireland,
Morrison Chambers, 32 Nassau Street, Dublin D02 YH68.

To my sister, Trudy

CONTENTS

Introduction
The Business of Creating Opportunities for
Yourself and for Others (without Stitching
Other Women Up) ———————————————— 1

Chapter 1
How to Own Your Ambition ————————— 23

Chapter 2
How to Promote Yourself (without Making
Everyone Want to Punch You in the Face) ——— 47

Chapter 3
How to Network and Meet Other People
(without Wanting to Hide under a Table) ——— 67

Chapter 4
How to Make Sure You (and Other Women)
Get Paid What You Deserve ————————— 89

Chapter 5
How to Conquer 'Hepeating' and Being
Interrupted in Meetings ——————————— 107

Chapter 6
How to Get Mentoring Right ———————— 133

Chapter 7
How to Own Up to Your Mistakes and Help
Others to Own Up to Theirs ———————— 155

Chapter 8
How to Support Other Women (without
Disappearing Yourself) ——————————— 175

Chapter 9
How to Handle Rivalry ——————————— 193

Chapter 10
How to Reach Out for Help (Elegantly),
Especially When You Fear Rejection ————— 211

Chapter 11
How to Recruit Allies (Hello, Men) ————— 227

Conclusion
The Business of Finding Your Own Path
Through All This (and Making Peace with
Not Being the Perfect Sister) ———————— 247

Further Reading ————————————— 255

Acknowledgements ——————————— 261

INTRODUCTION

The Business of Creating Opportunities for Yourself and for Others (without Stitching Other Women Up)

'Empowering women doesn't come from selfishness but rather from selflessness'

Selene Kinder, founder of Empowering Women Now

Where does the idea of 'lift as you climb' come from? I wish I could pretend that I thought of it. But that would be a lie. The expression has been around for over a hundred years. Although the identity of the person who first used these words is not certain, we have a pretty good idea of who it might have been. Mary Church Terrell was an African American activist who championed racial equality and votes for women in the late nineteenth century. Known as 'Mollie' by her family, she was born in 1863 in Memphis and her parents were freed slaves. She was one of the first African American women to earn a college degree. Her degree was in classics and she went on to teach Latin and modern languages before devoting her life to political activism.

Terrell was an accomplished public speaker and gave her speeches excellent straight-talking titles like 'In Union There Is Strength' and 'What It Means to Be

Colored in the Capital of the US'. But the expression with which she is most closely associated was the motto of the National Association of Colored Women, of which she was the first president. It's a great motto for life: 'Lifting As We Climb'. The women in this association strongly believed that by elevating themselves they could elevate other women and entire communities. Terrell might not have come up with those precise words herself but she would definitely have been in the room. And she spoke many times of the importance of elevating others. Indeed, we should think of her as a one-woman elevator. Something we should surely all aspire to be.

Since this expression first surfaced in 1896, the idea of 'lifting as you climb' has been used regularly for inspiration in both the women's movement and the human rights movement. It has frequently cropped up in corporate or philanthropic contexts, occasionally as a conference title or a T-shirt slogan. Maya Angelou referenced it regularly, sometimes overtly, sometimes with a touch of side-eye: 'I've learned that you shouldn't go through life with a catcher's mitt on both hands; you need to be able to throw something back.' More recently, the former US Secretary of State Madeleine Albright popularized a similar expression: 'There is a special place in hell for women who don't help each other.' Albright explained that 'women have an obligation to help one another'. In other words: if you don't lift as you climb, you know where you're going to end up.

The concept embodied by the twin ideas of 'lifting as you climb' and 'the special place in hell' has long been fascinating to me. We usually associate this sort of dutiful sisterhood with the rights and advancement of women. But, in the true spirit of Mary Church Terrell's original motto, these ideas really apply to us all as a society. When an individual achieves alone, especially when they do this at the expense of others, this is not real progress. In recent times the necessity to move forward together – and change things, sometimes radically, without leaving anyone behind – has taken on an urgency, in part as a result of the activism behind #MeToo and Black Lives Matter, not to mention the economic chaos unleashed on women's professional lives as a result of a global pandemic.

And yet it's somehow threatening instead of motivating, isn't it? To have the prospect of 'the special place in hell' held over you. It's a strange notion, this idea that not only is there something wrong with you if you are a woman and you do not help other women but also that you should be actively punished for not helping because it makes you a traitor. By extension, this means it's unnatural – immoral, even – for women to be ambitious only for themselves. They must be ambitious for all women or they will go to hell. As if this idea weren't scary enough, it coexists with the fact that no one seems to demand the same of men. Because men are not obliged to help other men. No one threatens to send them to hell for being selfish and go-getting. No one tells them to lift as they do all the climbing that seems to have worked out so well for them over the past few thousand years.

Another point of concern is that whenever I've heard these expressions referenced over the years, it's often by a woman who pays lip service to helping other women, loudly declaring herself 'such a feminist – it's my passion!' at every available opportunity whilst doing as much as possible to promote her own cause and absolutely nothing to promote anybody else's work. (Not you, former Secretary of State Albright. You are safe from the fires of hell, especially because you have an excellent collection of brooches.) So here's the thing. These 'lift as you climb' ambitions appear to be positive and fabulous. But in fact they are steeped in hypocrisy, narcissism, judgement, veiled threats and a weird misogyny: that you are a hateful woman if you're not enough of a sister.

When I first heard about the expression and began to look at how it relates to what I see around me, I started to worry about how this complex feminist intention can be defined, calibrated, measured. How much lifting is enough lifting? Does it count if you try to lift someone and you fail? What if the rung of the ladder that you are standing on snaps whilst you are trying to lift a sister up and you bring her down with you? Is there something a bit patronizing about trying to help other women who might be doing just fine on their own without your meddling help? Do you have to wait for someone to ask for your help or should you just offer it? What if someone asks you for help whom you find really annoying? Do you have to lift them too? As you can see, I have spent a lot of my time worrying about ending up in hell.

I was also acutely aware, when I was a little girl, that the one woman who did seem to have climbed as high as anyone possibly could and definitely had no fear of hell or any other place – Margaret Thatcher – made no secret of the fact that she did not believe in helping other women at all (terrible idea!) and that she did not expect anyone to help her either. I had the impression that if anyone did attempt to assist her in any way, she would bat them away with her handbag. The broadcaster Jenni Murray once recounted that in an interview with Mrs Thatcher she particularly pressed her on this point and the then Prime Minister replied: 'A woman must rise through merit. There must be no discrimination.' No lifting. Only climbing. Understood? When Murray tried to press her on how exactly she had held authority in situations where she was the only woman, Thatcher simply could not and would not respond. She often refused to acknowledge her gender and intimated that this stance was the definition of true equality. In the space between all these issues a certain mystery has taken hold as to what it means to be an ambitious woman who doesn't risk heading for the special place in hell.

Let's assume that most women agree broadly with Madeleine Albright and disagree with Margaret Thatcher. It would, of course, be great to think that everything happens on merit and there is no discrimination and only the best candidates rise to the top. If I were Margaret Thatcher (and for so many reasons, let's thank the heavens that I'm not), I would very much want to think this. It's interesting, isn't it, that it's often the people who reach the top who are most keen to say that it can't possibly be by fluke or accident or luck or coincidence or by virtue of them having recruited the right people to help them or because they had a hairstyle that was really popular at the time. Their success must simply be because they are brilliant.

Thirty years after Margaret Thatcher left office, though, I think it's safe to say that most of us recognize that success doesn't just 'happen'. It's all part of a system. And it's very hard to conquer that system on your own. I'm obviously not talking about getting ahead in politics here. Or rising to the top of the Conservative party. I'm talking about the system that is life. Most of us have at the very least a tacit acknowledgement that we are going to need some lifting as we climb. And that we would quite like to help others on our journey. But we rarely talk about what this actually looks like and how we can make it happen.

Why we need altruistic self-help

Yes, my fellow pedants, I realize that 'altruistic self-help' is a contradiction in terms, but it's an idea that makes perfect sense when you start to think about what it means to lift as you climb. What's the point of thinking about this concept? Why not just write a book about ambition and the best ways to screw everyone else over whilst building yourself a marble bathroom with gold taps, amassing the biggest collection of designer shoes and getting everyone to have sex with you and only you? Now that I've written it down, that does actually sound like a book I would like to read ... But, no, I don't think that is what any of us really want. I think we want to achieve things in life – all kinds of things, from the admirable and the philanthropic to the frivolous and the materialistic. But most of us do not want to achieve those things at the expense of others. And we definitely don't want to risk going to hell. If recent history has taught us anything (hello, covid-19), then it is that we have so much more responsibility to each other than many of us perhaps ever imagined. This is about finding a way to stay fierce, committed and hopeful without using our ambition, focus and optimism to screw over other people as well as the planet. Maybe this is my lockdown-era inner Dalai Lama talking, but lately I've become convinced that for the past few decades working life was too much about quantity, speed and progress, and not enough about quality, long-lasting results and long-term consequences. I shudder when I think about the motto Mark Zuckerberg used to found Facebook: 'Move fast and break things.' What would it be like if we followed the advice of this African proverb instead? 'If you want to go fast, go alone. If you want to go far, go together.'

This, then, is self-help but with the eventual goal of helping others. Altruistic self-help, if you like. Or alternative self-help. Because 'self-help' is all very well and good, but the clue is in the word itself: it's about helping your own little self, not anyone else. And ultimately there is something narcissistic, short-termist and – let's be honest – *selfish* about that. It's interesting how we don't really question that very obvious connection between 'selfish' and 'self-help'; we just ask whether a particular piece of advice is going to help us and help us right now. We don't ask whether it is going to change us long term and simultaneously benefit others. But what is the point in changing (or 'helping') ourselves – and this is almost always not about help but about change – if it is not for the benefit of others too? We don't try to understand our lives and make changes because we want to change in isolation and be the only amazing person in the world. We want to change in relation to, and alongside, our fellow humans. We are social animals. We want to rub along better with other people. We want to help others and know how to ask for help ourselves. All without being made to feel helpless and needy. That all sounds lovely and warm and fuzzy, doesn't it? And it is. Helping others whilst helping yourself is a good thing.

But this plan is also about good old-fashioned individualistic self-help. It has to be. Because unless you can climb, by helping yourself, you cannot lift anyone else. That said, I personally don't really like the idea of 'climbing' as a goal in itself. It suggests 'climbing the greasy pole' or 'being a social climber' or 'working your way up the career ladder', and all these things are ideas that make me want to start a hippy commune where I farm my own almond milk. But we have to be realistic and hold some of our reservations lightly. Before we can lift, we must know how to climb. You can't separate the two. And if lifting and climbing are good enough for the ladies in Mary Church Terrell's world, then lifting and climbing are good enough for me.

A space in between self-care and caring about others

Historically, until relatively recently, it was often unwise for women to be ambitious or out for themselves. At best, they would be harshly judged. At worst they would be ostracized. As Professor Mary Beard has pointed out in her work on power, until the last 150 years there were very few leadership roles women could publicly occupy. For many centuries, in the Western world the only prominent female role at the top of the ladder was that of the

Queen. Also, for both men and women, until the twenti-eth century most people considered that the role (and class) they were born into was their lot in life. It was very difficult to transcend social class, especially for women. 'Social mobility' – still a contentious issue – is a modern phenomenon. Climbing was in and of itself perilous, and often pointless. There was simply too much that counted against you.

In the last century, however, a lot has changed. Edu-cation, literacy and feminism have exposed the outdated lie that 'leadership is masculine'. Since the Second World War and in particular since the second wave of feminism in the 1960s, women in progressive societies have been taught to dismiss these old ideas and just go for it. You are now seen as a bit of a weakling if you don't embrace your ambition. Any career hesitations you might be experiencing are written off as 'imposter syndrome'. And yet. So many women – even those with a lot of advantages and privileges in terms of opportunity, tal-ent and education – seem to feel held back and unable to pursue their ambition. A lot of us seem to feel uncom-fortable around the idea of 'ambition' and 'climbing' and much of that has to do with the fact that we don't talk openly about how to integrate the 'lifting' into our goals. And without the 'lifting' bit, many women don't really want to do any of it – they're simply not in the game. Not because we are scared to be out for ourselves. That criti-cism can just be written off as misogynistic. No. We get scared because no one really wants to do anything in isolation. First because it isn't right; it doesn't feel natural. And second because it's lonely. What's the point in getting to the top if you're up there on your own? Defining a new kind of ambition, then, is about exploring the messy space in between what Gwyneth Paltrow might call 'self-actualization' (done for your own benefit) and what Greta Thunberg might call 'social change' (done for the benefit of all).

The first part of the altruistic self-help paradox is self-development, self-actualization, self-fulfilment – whatever you want to call it. It's about defining your own ambition. Some people might call it working on your 'personal brand'. The inverted commas are intentional. Clearly, 'personal brand' is a thing, but it doesn't have to be a thing that we are entirely comfortable with. I don't think 'personal brand' has to be completely toxic (and in some spheres it's unavoidable) but I do think it's something to be wary of. Naturally, women, as well as men, should strive for money and power and status and all these supposedly good things. But no human being should achieve those things at the expense of their humanity. And sometimes this 'personal brand' idea strays a long way towards people treating themselves like a commodity to be monetized. This can't be healthy, and a lot of criticism is levelled at the self-help industry, the cult of personal branding and the fad for 'self-care'. These phenomena are seen as self-serving, preening and self-absorbed. Some of this is justified. When we are focused only on ourselves we can be blind to the cares of others. But it's also true that you cannot do anything for anyone else unless you are relatively stable yourself. The more at ease you are with your own problems, the more generous you are able to be with other people.

The second part of the paradox is an acknowledgement that there is no point in doing anything if you are only doing it for selfish reasons. It's the reason to guard against becoming too much of a personal brand or becoming only a personal brand. Sure, climb. Find the most efficient and exciting way to climb. But think about lifting while you do it. There's a lot to be said for pitching yourself between these two extremes. As Tolstoy said: 'Everyone thinks of changing the world, but no one thinks of changing himself.' The world is changed faster if we all change as individuals ('climb') and then take others with us ('lift').

In reality, these two extremes (egotism versus altruism) are not really opposites. They are part of a dance. Yes, this is a plea for more dancing. Who doesn't need more dancing? The other bonus to this two-pronged approach - balancing your own goals with thinking about how you can serve other people - is that it's a much more effective way of looking after yourself. The recent obsession with 'self-care' has led us away from the most obvious piece of advice for anyone who is feeling down or lonely: often the thing most likely to pull us out of a depressive or anxious episode is a conversation with someone else. Self-care does not have to mean locking yourself away and applying an organic clay mask. I always have a bit of a word with myself if ever I am feeling down about all the pressures of adult life: 'Viv,' I ask, 'have you had any in-depth conversations with any of your friends lately?' If the answer is no, then it's time to go for a drink and a chat with the people who love you. Because if you scratch the surface, guess what? We're all dealing with the same insecurities and difficulties. Sharing these concerns with others and working out a way forward is heartening. Step away from the clay mask. (Obviously, do apply the clay mask if you really want to. Just don't imagine that it is really going to benefit your soul or your career.)

By concentrating less on self-care and more on other people, it's surprisingly easy to find other people who also have sick elderly parents, stroppy teenagers and/or power-crazed, infantile bosses in their lives. And/or a massive mortgage. And/or an inability to get out of the horrible rental they're living in. It amuses me that in all the advice that is given about 'self-care', no one ever advises that *Schadenfreude* (taking joy in others' misery) is actually one of the best forms of medicine there is. A benign form of *Schadenfreude* can be really useful. It's a reminder that there is always someone worse off than you. Gratitude lists are very popular these days, and I don't dismiss the idea of writing down the things that you are thankful for – quite the opposite – because there is scientific evidence that counting your blessings does help with the balance of your mental health. But I often wonder about other methods that might be equally useful. Like keeping a list of people who are worse off than you. Cutting pictures out of the newspapers of car crashes that you weren't involved in. Storing some screenshots on your phone of skin diseases that you don't have. Perhaps you shouldn't literally do these things. I have no medical qualifications to suggest that these things will benefit you. But you get what I'm saying. It's helpful to focus on the positives.

Connection to others and recognizing where we are in the scheme of things is incredibly valuable. A simple example. Last summer whilst I was on holiday, on a beautiful sunny day sitting outside a cafe at a picture-perfect marketplace in Montpellier, I was feeling grumpy and sorry for myself because I had some really itchy mosquito bites and because I couldn't spend the whole day relaxing as I had a small amount of work to do. (Yes, I know. Boo hoo.) Whilst I was thinking about how terrible this was for me and what a great burden I bear in this life, three women in a row walked past me with varying kinds of fractured wrists. Now that I think about it, the simple explanation is that I was near a fracture clinic. But still. At the time I took it as a sign: 'What are you moaning about? At least you don't have a fractured wrist.' My next thought was: 'Usually when someone thinks something like this, it's just before they fall over and break their wrist.' So I walked very slowly and carefully back to my holiday home and quietly settled down to my work, humbled and lively of wrist, mosquito bites gently throbbing. The more opportunities we have to feel slightly humbled without feeling completely broken and humiliated, the better.

This kind of feeling – being grateful to be alive – is the right kind of self-care. There's much current talk of the flip side of the 'be-good-to-yourself' movement. Friends pulling out of arrangements because 'my mental health comes first'. Yes, of course it should. But so should your friends' mental health and the support they rely on from you. Friends not wanting to go out of their way to visit new mothers because 'my weekends are precious'. Yes, so they should be. But so is your relationship with an old friend who might have the early stirrings of post-natal depression but can't find a way to say that to you on WhatsApp or social media. We all need boundaries and time to ourselves and permission to be 'selfish'. We cannot look after others unless we put our own needs first. But we also need to recognize that this is a very delicate and ever-changing balance. And that putting ourselves first is not the end goal. It is a means to an end. You put yourself first so that you can be sorted enough and generous enough and calm enough to do things for others.

Disclaimer: a word about the difference between attitude and mental health

The ideas in this book are designed to make you feel challenged, fired up and inspired to find your own version of lifting and climbing. I am a practitioner of tough love and I do my best to tell it like it is. My way of thinking about how to manage work and life is influenced by my own experiences in and around different workspaces, by my life as a freelancer for twenty years and by interviewing – on and off the record – thousands of people over twenty-five years in journalism. In my everyday life, the way I see things is affected by my marriage of twenty years, my three children and my experiences of mental health challenges in my own life and in the lives of people I grew up with. In the last five years I've spent time coaching and workshopping with hundreds of women (and a lot of men) across different industries, and my approach can be blunt: if you don't change anything about yourself, nothing changes. There is no silver bullet. You have to get things wrong before you get them right. It's great to learn from other people but you can only really learn from your own mistakes. That said, it's very important to note that I am not a psychotherapist and I am not a doctor. I love encouraging people to pull themselves up by their bootstraps and get on with life. And I love reminding them that one of the most freeing things any of us can ever realize is that other people really do not care about us at all – in a good way. I mean this very much in the sense that they are not focused on us: they have their own concerns. I don't mean that they mean to be neglectful towards us. All I mean is that we really don't need to be so self-conscious, and we don't need to be so scared of making mistakes, because no one else is watching in quite the way we think they are. They have their own stuff going on.

However, none of this happy-clappy stuff is relevant if you are suffering from poor mental health. If you are experiencing clinical anxiety, depression, stress or any other condition and you are really struggling with life day to day, then you need professional help. You must get that help. You cannot be thinking about doing any climbing or lifting of any kind if you are not in good health. Be honest and patient with yourself about what you need. Some of us know instinctively when we need to give ourselves a pep talk and a dose of inspiration, when we need to improve our attitude. And we know instinctively when it's more serious and we need to consult a professional. Others need to ask friends or colleagues whether our judgement is sound. Saying something like this to someone you trust can go a long way: 'This is how I am feeling at the moment. Does it seem like I'm coping OK? Or do I need more help?'

There is a huge difference between someone suffer-ing from clinical anxiety (where medication and/or therapy is needed) and someone who feels anxious about their next work presentation or is stressed because they don't think they have enough LinkedIn contacts. If you have any doubt about your feelings and how serious they are, go and talk to a doctor or a counsellor. Similarly – in the spirit of 'lift as you climb' – watch out for poor mental health in other people. Do you have a colleague with long-term anxiety that isn't improving? Do you know if they have anyone to talk to? How can you take the pressure off other people around you who might be feeling stressed? I know from my own experiences that there are times when I need to improve my attitude and keep an eye on how I'm looking after myself (exercise, sleep, diet, avoiding overwork) and there are times when I need some other kind of intervention (in my case, therapy, which I have found incredibly useful).

This conversation about ambition is loosely designed to mimic career progression. The early chapters are about personal ambition and making your way in the world, with later chapters moving on to the idea of 'lifting' others once you've climbed a bit of a way yourself. Both aspects – climbing and lifting – require thought, practice and consideration. So at the end of each chapter I've included some ideas that should help you find solutions to the issues raised. Or at least give you a starting point and an outlet for your own feelings. You could go on to the next chapter without considering the points on the chapter you've just read. But in my experience of doing a lot of this kind of work and of self-reflection, it does help if you get your thoughts down on paper. If nothing else, you can have a good laugh at yourself further down the line. I find it hilarious – and depressing – to find 'goals' and 'issues' that I have written down to work on around ten years ago and compare them to what I might have written last week. It's usually the same old ideas, and often in the exact same words. We can be very slow to move on. So anything that can move us forward a teeny bit faster is a good thing. Any decent therapist will tell you that this is normal: frequently, in therapy, we don't sort out our issues until we have completely bored ourselves silly going over and over the same stuff.

I know that when I am not feeling great in myself, I am less able to help others or to even think about what I could do for someone else. This book is an exploration of what we can all do to find a balance in ourselves in order to be able to help each other. Because you cannot be generous to other people and help them climb if you are barely keeping your own head above water. You cannot be a role model, offer inspiration or show strength or leadership if your opinion of yourself is negative. You cannot be confident enough to talk about your vulnerabilities or difficulties if you are actually suffering because of those vulnerabilities and difficulties. (Well, you could, but it's pretty taxing and can be risky for your health.) And we really need people – especially women – to do all these things and be visible doing these things in order for the world to change. The point of this book? How to support yourself better so that you can support others.

1

How to Own Your Ambition

> '*I tell my students, "When you get these jobs that you have been so brilliantly trained for, just remember that your real job is that if you are free, you need to free somebody else. If you have some power, then your job is to empower somebody else. This is not just a grab-bag candy game."*'
> Toni Morrison

How do we work out what our personal ambitions are? How do we get comfortable with them? How do we use them for good? The idea is that by doing the exercises at the end of each chapter, you will find out (a) what your true ambitions are, (b) the steps you will need to take in order to achieve them and (c) how you can form those ideas and take those steps without treading on others. This book also might offer some answers as to why you feel uncomfortable around the idea of ambition or feel defensive about the assumption that ambition is 'bad'. And it might give you some insight into why you have have failed to realize some of your ambitions. This is an exploration of a topic which, with a dose of self-help, aims to act as a road map to 'good' ambition, whatever that means to you. If that sounds non-committal, it's because I am not interested in being judgemental about your goals. If your ambition is to put by enough money so that you can give up work and start a soup kitchen for the homeless or put by enough money so that you can give up work and re-watch every episode of *Love Island* fifty-seven times, then that's your call. Ambition can be channelled in whichever direction you want. What I am interested in – and, yes, a bit judgemental about – is the way you go about achieving your goals, thereby making sure you're able to sleep easy at night.

It's worth thinking about the preconceptions you might have about ambition. In the past the concept has often been associated with aggressive go-getting. How to Get to the Top. How to Bagsy the Corner Office. How to Network with the Right People So That You Can Get On. For too long, the idea of women's ambition has been tainted with a 1980s-shoulder-padded stereo-type about elbowing other people out of the way, building your personal brand and trampling whoever needs to be trampled to get to where you need to be. I'm not sure this was ever really a good way to go about doing things. Although it's a great narrative for a film or a novel, in real life things are more complicated. You have to navigate around people. You have to help others in order to help yourself – and often in an altruistic way, without knowing what (if anything) you will get in return. You have to learn to listen to and trust your instincts. And you have to learn to disregard the views of others if and when they are derailing you from what you want.

This is hard-fought knowledge for me. I grew up in the 1970s and 1980s in an environment where little girls were given conflicting messages about what was possible. On the one hand, I was frequently told that I could do anything I wanted in life and that as long as I got the best grades at school then nothing could hold me back. (No pressure, guys!) On the other hand, several adults in my childhood told me that being a writer was 'a pie-in-the-sky idea' and that the idea of writing books, working for magazines or being on television – all things I said I wanted to do from a young age – was 'a bit far-fetched'. I remember feeling confused about these mixed messages. On the one hand, ambition was encouraged and rewarded. As long as it fitted within the confines of the education system. On the other hand, too much ambition was frowned upon and could lead to you being very disappointed. And if you had lofty goals, then you should probably not tell people about them because they will think that you are egotistical and 'getting above yourself'. I recently found out about the American expression 'Don't get above your raisin'.' This is their equivalent of 'Don't get ideas above your station.' Lots of us imbibed that idea as girls without anyone ever having to mention raisins.

A lot of this thinking – about certain professions being difficult to get into or needing to know the right people – has collapsed in the face of the digital revolution. If I had had the internet as a child, then I could have Googled 'How do you get published as a writer?' and realized that it's not so pie-in-the-sky after all. As it was, I had absolutely no idea how being published happened and, perhaps more crucially, no one to ask. So it was easy for me to believe that it was a very difficult thing to achieve, maybe impossible. I saw no evidence to the contrary. Now we live in a world where not only is it ridiculously easy to find out anything about anything in less than a second but it is also easy to do anything you want for yourself, rather than waiting for someone to give you permission. You don't even need to know how the traditional publishing process works; you can publish your own book, start your own TV channel, run your own multimedia platform from social media networks. The big question is no longer just about your ambition, but how you want to go about achieving it. And from there, do you want to do it on your own or with the help of others? What does success look like for you?

So why do so many of us still struggle to be comfortable with the idea of owning our own ambition? In some ways the twenty-first-century set-up makes 'ambition' easier than it has ever been before: You know what you want? Go and do it. No one is stopping you. Especially if you are self-motivated. In other ways, though, it has up-ended logic and reason and driven us half mad. As human beings, we love to be approved of and acknowledged by others. This isn't just a narcissistic trait. (Although obviously it can be when this need is excessive.) It's a basic human need. We like others to choose us and give us their seal of approval. We like to matter to other people. In a professional sense, we want gatekeepers and employers and bosses to tell us that we're doing the right thing and that we should continue doing it. In a community sense, we want to know that we have a role and that people would miss us if we weren't here.

In a world where the gatekeepers are disappearing, how you define ambition becomes increasingly difficult. It also reveals what we assign meaning to. Is it meaningful to accumulate 10,000 followers? Is that the right kind of ambition? Or it is better to have a boss who tells you that you're doing a great job? Or does only simultaneously having both those things count as success? Can a social media presence that goes viral replace the buzz of being part of a community where you have a certain reputation and standing? I think having so many ideas of what ambition might be means that it's harder than ever for us to know what it means to be 'ambitious' and what our personal 'ambition' is. There are no excuses any more – that 'It's not for the likes of me,' or 'I don't know the right people,' or 'I have no idea how to make that happen.' Having all the choice in the world and no excuses is hard.

At the same time, in the Western world our moral universe has been completely transformed over the past fifty years. When my grandmother was growing up, her mother ran a pub and a shop; my great-grandmother Beatrice had no ambitions other than to keep food on the table. In turn, my grandmother Vera also ran a shop (something she wasn't especially proud of, I think, although she wasn't ashamed either – her grocery store was an excellent shop). One of her great-est ambitions had been to be highly educated – to go to university, for example – and to teach. She was schooled to the age of eighteen and taught briefly before she got married. It was an achievement that remained with her for the rest of her life. I am proud of her, too, given her upbringing. And I'm proud of that grocery store which she ran with my grandfather. But if I had had to live her life . . . Well, I would have torched the premises a long time ago. Because she infected me with very different kinds of ambition: travel, inde-pendence, freedom, education, creativity. Ambitions change, and our ideas of what is possible, and whether we have the capacity to pursue those ambitions, change with each passing generation.

With all this comes freedom. And with freedom comes responsibility. The idea of 'analysis paralysis' or 'overchoice' or 'choice overload' has been prevalent in psychological thinking since the 1970s. This is the idea that in a consumer society where most people are educated and not held back by assumptions about class, race or gender (ahem, yes, I know), making decisions about our lives becomes a cognitive burden. Put simply, we don't always have the mental bandwidth to deal with the huge decisions that we have to make. If we form an ambition and it doesn't work out, then we have no one to blame but ourselves. Arguably, it would be much simpler to be like my grandmother and just have to work in the shop because nothing else is available. There has never been a better time, then, for us to support each other in our complicated, hard-won ambitions, to own them, talk them through and work out how we are going to make them happen. We can make each other accountable, make sure we're not holding ourselves back and look collectively at the external forces that are still making progress difficult for many women.

The importance of knowing your own mind

One thing I have learned over the years, as a journalist interviewing all kinds of people from different walks of life, from answering the questions of hundreds of listeners who wrote in to the (now sadly retired) *Dear Viv* agony-aunt podcast, talking to thousands of women at events connected to my book *How to Own the Room*, and as a performance coach, is that a great many people face the same handful of issues at work. We all think that what we do in our jobs is so specific. But in fact the questions that crop up around ambition in the workplace are the same. How can you 'fix' a person who is blocking you at work? How can you ask for a promotion or more money? Should you leave a job that you hate? How can you get your brilliance noticed? What do you do if someone keeps interrupting you in meetings? Everyone wants, more or less, the same things. And often these are to do with wishing that they could control other people's behaviour.

But whilst we all might have common aims (an interesting life, a fulfilling job, work–life balance, financial comfort . . .) and we often have common problems (difficult bosses, lack of flexibility, annoying colleagues . . .), how we respond to these things needs to be intensely personal. You can't effect change by adopting just one course of action. This is not a one-size-fits-all fix. It depends where your ambition lies. And it depends where you work. The solutions can be very industry-specific. Some life paths involve the cultivation of extreme, hard-nosed ambition. Others are far more relaxed and fluid. It's important to try to choose a path that fits you as a person and matches with your own definition of ambition.

So, for example, one question that comes up a lot

when I'm presenting at a corporate event is what to do if you don't know the answer to a question. What do you do if you are in a situation at work and you are exposed as ignorant or stupid? This could happen if you're talking on a panel, if you're in the middle of a broadcast discussion, if you're at a job interview or if you're giving an important presentation at work. Or, more generally, if someone senior puts you on the spot and you have to disappoint them. My own advice would be either to be honest or to style it out. You could say, 'I don't know the answer to that but I do know who I can ask . . .' or, 'I don't know the answer to that but my educated guess would be . . .' Because I am not answerable to anyone in my work, it's OK for me simply to say, 'I don't know.' In fact, it's probably good for me to say that because it's pointless me pretending that I know the answer to something when I don't.

However, there are many industries where this response is categorically impossible. This question came up when I was doing an event for the financial sector and I realized from the intake of breath in the audience that this was a sackable offence. My usual advice to style it out was not going to wash. A senior woman piped up: 'All you can do is say, "I should know the answer to that but I don't have it to hand. Let me get it to you as soon as this meeting is finished."' In another walk of life, where creativity is important, the ability to say 'I don't know' may be celebrated or even admired.

In banking, however, forget it. You need to have a high level of traditional ambition to work in that sector. And you need to feel comfortable working in a place where it's culturally unacceptable to admit you're wrong. Or you could make it your ambition to change that culture. If you are extremely patient and resourceful.

So there are no off-the-peg answers in this book. One person's elegant fudge is another's P45. What I am able to do is give you some ideas and some inspiration to find the courage to navigate your own way. Many women who I have worked with have had to find the confidence to figure things out for themselves without relying on any blueprint. Sometimes they have been the first women to blaze a trail in their industries or in their companies. Sometimes they have had to copy men to get ahead because there is no one else to copy. Sometimes they have done the complete opposite to what everyone else around them is doing either to stand out or to try something different and find out what happens. The point is: none of this is easy. Anyone who says it is easy is lying. But the way to make it really difficult for yourself is to do it on your own, be scared of everything, ignore the fact that you need to work on your resilience and bravery – and assume that someone else must know the perfect answer and the shortcut. If they do – and, I would guess, mostly they don't – they most likely figured it out by accident or are about to fall flat on their face.

Why ambition can be difficult to define

It's worth remembering the origin of the word 'ambition'. It comes from the Latin noun *ambitio*, which derives from the verb *ambulare* – 'to walk around'. 'Ambitio' was used to describe the walk taken around the public space where voters in elections would be gathered. It came to mean 'ambition for political office'. So, originally, ambition was focused on the idea of winning popularity and getting people to vote for you, what we would now call 'canvassing' or 'electioneering'. By extension, it also meant 'striving for advancement'. Interestingly, these concepts are even less attractive than the idea of 'ambition'. (In Roman law a related term took on a more negative tinge still: *ambitus* meant 'a crime of political corruption'.) Few of us want to admit to ourselves, let alone to others, that we want to be popular or that we want to advance ourselves. Or that we would corrupt ourselves to gain advantage. On the other hand, some people can get quite aggressive about wanting to rebrand ambition as a positive thing because they think that seeing it as a 'dirty word' holds us all back. Others embrace ambition in a contrarian and defiant way: 'I'm unashamedly ambitious.' The word is surrounded by baggage. It's never neutral. In some ways, the original derivation means: 'I want to lead.' No wonder that until very recently people have been uncomfortable around the idea of women and ambition.

Ambition means completely different things to different people. One person's idea of ambition is another person's idea of flaky and limiting. Some of us are ambitious for money and power. Some are ambitious for a balanced family life. Others are ambitious about achieving peace and quiet. Some people think they can use their ambition to achieve all these things at once. (Good luck with that.) The word 'ambition' becomes a catch-all for 'getting what you want out of life'. And that, of course, is something that changes constantly over the course of our lives and is also redefined according to what's going on around us. So 'ambition' is a tricky beast to pin down because its meaning is neither clear nor shared. And also because negative connotations are frequently attached to it, especially for women.

It can also be a massive red herring that holds you back, particularly if you misunderstand the context you're operating in. Back in the 1980s, there was a very fixed idea of what 'ambition' meant and we were supposed to embrace it. It was about doing well at school and then somehow mysteriously creating opportunities for yourself. It was about setting your sights as high as you possibly could and not 'settling'. It took me many years to recognize that this is not as easy as it sounds. Sometimes we don't know what opportunity looks like until we get closer to it. We often make mistakes in our thinking about what is ambitious and what isn't. For example, one of the first massive hurdles in my career was caused by a major error in the feminist thinking at my school. This was a result of a huge misunderstanding of what ambition is and how it is constantly being redefined.

When I was in my mid teens, the headmistress of my school decreed that no girls in the school should be taught how to touch-type. In her mind this made sense because she did not want girls deciding that a secretarial job was the height of their ambition. In theory, this seems like a noble edict. Why raise children who limit themselves? She did not want classes of schoolleavers who were going straight into secretarial jobs. She wanted us to go to university and become scientists or captains of industry. We would have our own secretaries. (Let's not get into the fact that this policy was not exactly empowering of the other women who would have to do our admin for us. They would be from other schools, so that would be their problem, not ours.)

You can guess what was coming next, though. The advent of the personal computer, the invention of the internet, a world where no one has a secretary any more anyway and a world where the touch-typers have inherited the earth: social media. The school policy intended to get us to set our sights higher left us woefully underqualified for modern life and really for any job, let alone one as a secretary. After university I went for an editorial assistant job on *Esquire* magazine. I applied, only to find out that one of the job requirements was a typing speed of at least sixty words per minute on a QWERTY keyboard. I managed to get the job, but only just. I nearly didn't get it because I couldn't type fast enough. One of the main requirements of my role was to input copy from the writers, who would send in their articles by fax. (Fortunately, email was invented about two years later and this part of my job was discontinued.) I had to be sent on a special training course to learn how to touch-type. These sessions were before work, at 6.30 a.m. every day, until my typing was fast enough. I am eternally grateful for that course because my ability to type quickly is a skill I use every day. It's maybe the most valuable skill I have and without it any other ambitions I might develop in life would be totally unattainable.

This is the danger of defining what 'ambition' constitutes. It needs to be a very informed definition – and perhaps involve some ability to see into the future. Similarly, I remember teachers at my school and university being slightly horrified that I was doing unpaid work experience on a women's magazine after I graduated. Everything I was doing there seemed to be uniquely unambitious: I was making tea and coffee, doing hours of photocopying and taking orders for toast which involved running back from the cafe with it so that the butter was still melting on the toast. I was twenty-two, I had a degree from Cambridge and spoke four languages – and this *Devil Wears Prada* stuff is what I was doing with my life? When I got my first byline in a magazine, it was an 'interview' with a prizewinning bull about his semen output. I am being serious. (I was asked to interview the owner and then write it up as if the bull were speaking because this would be 'hilarious'. This was not my idea.) My first paid piece for a magazine – for which I received £50 – was 'Man of the Month', which involved interviewing two of my ex-boyfriends and suggesting that people wrote in for dates with them. (This was also not my idea. One of them later revealed that he was gay.) A university tutor saw this article and was horrified.

It's true that none of this was particularly edifying or even remotely ambitious. Or was it? I did these things out of instinct, thinking that they would somehow lead to something. And they did. At the same time that all this was going on, I was working with one woman who went on to give me a column on a national newspaper several years later and with another who ended up as the first woman editor of the *Guardian*. I still work with her now, over twenty years later. (I hasten to say that neither of these women required the hot buttered toast, nor were they involved in anything to do with the semen-producing bull or the gay ex-boyfriend.) This is a roundabout way of saying that ambition is not always what it seems. Sometimes it looks like hot buttered toast. Or a talking bull whose prizewinning sperm is marketed around the world.

There is no magic bullet

This book is not a cure-all. But hopefully it is a mental oasis where you can think about some of these grey areas, how you feel about them and what you want to do about them. It is definitely not another excuse to give yourself a list of things to beat yourself up about. (As in: 'I'm not lifting enough other women! I haven't climbed far enough!') And it isn't a self-righteous plea to support the sisterhood at all costs. Because I know I have been personally lacking on that front many times. I can already sense some people reading this and screaming, 'But, Viv, women have been doing things for other people selflessly and without any thanks for thousands of years and look how that's worked out. It's time for the revolution! Tell women to put themselves first!' This is a good point. But I think we're all grown-up enough to understand the nuance here. And to realize that there are different times in all our lives for different motivations.

Our ambitions change all the time and we need to revisit them constantly. This is normal. One ambition can easily fade. Because you achieved it. Because when you got closer to it, it turned out to be not what you wanted. Or just because you changed. Equally our capacity to lift and help others achieve their ambitions varies dramatically over the course of our lives. There may be times when you are not really able to be there for others. Times when you have to be careful that you don't break promises or let down people who are relying on you. And you will recognize those particular moments when you are not at your best because you are tired or stressed or have too many family commitments. That is OK. That is a moment when you don't have to lift or climb; you can just collapse for a bit. It's like Salma Hayek once told Renée Zellweger: 'The rose doesn't bloom all year round. Unless it's plastic.' Salma was talking about physical health and aesthetic appearance. ('You can't look totally fabulous all the time, dahling. Give yourself a break.') But it's also true of our internal makeup. There are times when we have the internal strength that makes us able to put ourselves out there and forge on and make progress. And there are times when we need to hibernate and recalibrate. This is the time when it's fine to do the self-care/clay-mask thing.

Putting a name to your ambition is important. Lifting as you climb is not about suggesting that you abandon all thoughts of personal advancement and devote yourself to the cause of feminism. I love Madeleine Albright and she's right about hell. But at the same time, we really don't need another task that we feel obligated to perform. We should help others because we want to and because it's the right thing to do. We shouldn't do it because we are afraid of being roasted by the flames of Satan. We can list, know and own our ambitions because they are what will shape our lives.

CLIMB

● Do you have reservations or feelings of discomfort around the word 'ambitious'? Would you hate to be called ambitious? If so, it's worth rethinking this. Write a list of negative qualities you associate with ambitious people. ('They will do anything to succeed.' 'They trample over others to get what they want.' 'They only care about money.') Let out all your negative associations. Write ten or twenty sentences. Now look at the list and think about what a 'good' kind of ambition might look like and define that. So next to 'They will do anything to succeed', you could write: 'They have their limits like any other person.' Next to 'They trample over others', you could write: 'Healthily ambitious people want success for others as much as for themselves.' The point is obvious: you get to define what ambition means. You don't have to buy into some negative, externally defined idea.

● Make a list of things that you could do in your life but probably won't because they seem over-ambitious. This is a really, really useful list to hang on to. This exercise brings ideas into your mind that are lurking in your subconscious. Usually we don't let these ideas out because they seem like 'too much'. Let them out and see what they look like. Some people find it useful to do this exercise with money. How much money would you earn if you allowed yourself to be 'too ambitious'? Put a realistic number on what that might look like in your field. What are the things you would need to do in order to get to that number? Are they really out-landish ambitions? Or just steps that you could take over time?

● It's good to know what your ambitions are and to go for it but it's also good to remember that it's OK to be ambitious for peace of mind, for rest, for good physical and mental health. Put balance and sanity at the heart of your ambition. And remember to let yourself off the hook: lifting as you climb, defining your goals and try-ing to move forward should be empowering and liberating (as well as hard work). Be careful that they don't become another stick with which to beat your-self. The goals and the ambition should serve you – you are not serving them, just for the sake of looking busy and like a 'boss lady'. Social media is full of unhappy, overachieving boss ladies.

LIFT

● If you have no problem with the words 'ambition' or 'ambitious' then think about using them in association with yourself and other women in a positive context. We rarely describe others we admire as 'ambitious' unless it's to suggest that they are over-ambitious.

Praise women you know for their ambition and make it clear you see it as a positive attribute.

● If you have an opportunity as a leader or a manager to encourage other women to shape and voice their ambitions, then do it. We've all been in front of younger colleagues who have voiced crazy ambitions that are completely out of their grasp: listen patiently and do not laugh. I can remember being in an interview for a job on a magazine when I was in my early twenties and the editor asked me, 'Who would you want to see on the cover of the magazine?' I said, 'Madonna.' (This was a very good idea at the time, I promise.) She laughed scornfully and said, 'And how do you propose we make that happen?' The answer I had given was 'too ambitious' because I did not have a personal hotline to Madonna and could not make this cover interview happen. Everyone else in the meeting laughed at my naivety. I didn't get the job. About a year later one of the magazine's rivals had a huge cover story on Madonna as a result of the film *Evita*, an interview which could have been available to anyone who put in the best idea and the best offer. They needn't have laughed. I was right. (Not that I'm smug about it. OK, I'm smug about it.)

● When you see friends, colleagues or any women you know selling themselves short, say so. Pull other women up on the moments when they self-deprecate.

Remind them to always ask for more money and a better title, even if it's just to practise asking and accepting the risk of rejection. Encourage them to ask for more, dream bigger, be mildly outrageous in their demands. And ask them to hold you to the same standard.

● This is about social mobility, diversity and inclusion as much as it is about feminism. If you have the ability to encourage anyone who comes into your orbit to be more ambitious, do it. Lots of places need people to go in and talk about ambition, to mentor, to deliver inspirational talks: schools, sixth forms, colleges, universities, charities, mentoring groups. If you have already nailed your ambitions, think how you can volunteer to help others cultivate theirs.

2

How to Promote Yourself (without Making Everyone Want to Punch You in the Face)

*'The more you praise and celebrate your life,
the more there is in life to celebrate.'*
Oprah Winfrey

A lot has been said in the past ten years about women not having to apologize for who they are. We all know this new narrative. We must feel comfortable taking up space. We must not hide our light under a bushel. We must shout about our achievements. We must not allow ourselves to be held back by patriarchal dismissal of our contributions, of our bodies and of our life choices. All of this makes sense and it's right. It's a necessary corrective after centuries of women being told to put up and shut up, and of course it's something that is still going on in many parts of the world, which is why we owe it to ourselves even more to respect and use our freedom.

However, this attitude does have its limits. And we rarely talk about them, even though we are, I think, acutely aware of them and most women - almost all women - really, really, really do not want to come across as assholes. And yet how do you self-promote – especially on social media – and not come across as an insufferable self-promoter? It was one thing when our accounts of ourselves were confined to job applications, CVs or conversations at conferences. It's quite another when we are forced to make decisions about how public to be, how boastful to be, how modest to be on social media, 24/7. We all want to find a way of defining our limits. To find a way of saying and doing enough to keep employers and colleagues happy – and of maximizing our chances of success. But also to find a way of being authentic, maintaining our integrity and being able to sleep at night.

In the world of social media there's a convenient, self-serving excuse for being overly self-promoting and excessively narcissistic: 'Women spend too much time apologizing for promoting their work.' There is a truth to this. Women do spend too much time apologizing for highlighting their achievements. We should all probably self-promote a little more. But it's a balance. It's not an excuse to rewrite the mistakes of the past ('Be modest and unnoticeable, dear ladies!') with an over-correction ('Here are 1,754 pictures of me winning a trophy I awarded to myself').

This kind of faux 'You go, girl!' bravado is celebrated on social media and in some social and professional circles. It's an attitude that is symptomatic of a new kind of feminism which emerged about twenty years ago. This is the feminism that says: 'An action has been undertaken by a woman. The sheer fact that the action was undertaken by a woman makes it right.' In theory, I like this because it's laughably megalomaniac. In reality, it's reverse patriarchy and it's horrible. For centuries, it was fine to do most things simply because you were a man. And that was wrong. Now that things are changing, it's not OK to assume that just because you are a woman you get to hide behind the impact of your actions. This is true of ambition and it's also true of self-promotion. You can go too far with both of these things. And it's not OK to say, 'I can go as far as I like because I am a woman and women have been held back for centuries.'

That said, most women are, in my experience, the complete opposite of the sort of 'influencers' who burden the digital sphere with constant, empty achievement. Most women would rather chew their own arm off than purchase social media followers or catalogue their every moment of positive feedback. What they want to know is how they can be more bold about publicizing their achievements without straying into the territory of being the sort of person who boasts of greatness but is really not that great. Follower-buying is an extreme example of the perils of self-promotion, of course, and one which is way beyond anything most people are living through. But I think it's an example of what some of us fear. If we put ourselves on Instagram Stories, will people think we're trying to be an 'influencer'? Are we OK with that or are we horrified by it? If we do a weekly Facebook Live that only five people watch, are we pathetic? Or are we a bold, strong woman refusing to be silenced? These are questions to which each of us can only know our own subjective answer. For some people, social media is and always will be a massive cringe. For others, it's liberating and fun. The trick is to know your own mind and be willing to experiment to find the right level for you. One useful rule of thumb on social media is to ask yourself: 'Is this something I would celebrate with friends or colleagues in real life?' If it is a piece of news that's worthy of social celebration offline, it will work online without appearing gratuitous. And let's face it, the side of us that joins others online to applaud and celebrate is a side to cultivate.

Unsurprisingly, because social media is built on the politics of envy and aspiration, a lot of questions come up in relation to it which are really to do with not wanting to be the last person to the party. Or they're connected to people thinking, 'I really *should* be on Instagram/YouTube/Snapchat.' No. You shouldn't do anything that isn't fun or meaningful for you. You certainly shouldn't hold yourself back from trying new things because of fear or ignorance. But, equally, no one should feel forced to have some kind of stellar presence online or always be engaged in performative success-signalling for its own sake.

Certainly, people feel obliged to do all sorts of things that they are really not interested in at all. I have lost count of the number of people who want me to talk to them about podcasting because they think they should be making a podcast. To me this is the equivalent of saying, 'Please tell me about how you send a text. I need to send more texts.' If you want to send a text, send a text. If you want to make a podcast, make a podcast. It's really not difficult to find out 'how to make a podcast'. A much more important question is *why*. Why are you making a podcast? As a hobby? To promote yourself? Because it's a fun challenge? To fix a problem you've diagnosed? If so, can you afford to solve this problem for free? No? Ah, so you're doing this to make money? If so, what's your monetization model? How many hours a week are you going to spend making (i.e. working for free on) this podcast? How will you tell if it is 'successful'? How will you define 'successful'? People do not continue this conversation with me for very long.

But you get my point. We put ourselves under a ridiculous amount of pressure ('I should have a podcast; everyone has a podcast') without thinking about the practicalities and the realities. The truth of podcasts is that people are making them either out of passion for the medium, because it complements other areas of their work, because someone is paying them to or because they have false hope for things that might come from it but probably never will. This is also the truth about a huge amount of social media activity. Which is not to say that podcasts, social media, blogging, networking or promoting yourself using any social media method is pointless. Some of these things have been life-changing for people. It is to say this: we all need to trust our own instincts better around social media and learn to define our own individual limits and goals.

'But what if I look like a fake?'

Self-promotion has mushroomed beyond all belief in the past five years with the growth of social media and micro-blogging. Ten or twenty years ago we used to give each other advice about 'not being afraid to blow your own trumpet' (generally not a bad piece of advice, especially if you are the sort of person who self-deprecates too much). But now the opportunity to blow the trumpet is available 24/7, it has become a completely different game. We live in a world where it's extremely easy to make yourself look more impressive than you are, to conjure up an exciting and glamorous image online (and, to some extent, in real life). Women are frequently applauded for 'stepping up', 'pushing the boundaries' or 'refusing to be held back'. That's all great if it's authentic. But if it's built on a ton of fakery, we all lose when we become aware of these tales of hubris. The big question for all of us is how do we 'fake it' without being fake? Because we all have days when we don't feel like the CV version of ourselves.

I think it's important to break this issue into two categories. The first is how you talk to people in day-to-day life and in face-to-face interactions. This could be everything from what you say in a job interview to foreground your knowledge and experience, right through to how to describe your life of the past twenty years to people at a school reunion. (Side note: do not go to reunions. Life is too short.) The second area is the online space. This, unfortunately, cannot be avoided in the modern world.

Online and offline self-promotion have one thing in common: they depend on how self-conscious you are. And your level of self-consciousness is intimately linked to the factor that affects your entire attitude towards how you represent yourself: how much we care about other people. I cannot state strongly enough how important it is to care deeply about other people, whilst caring as little as possible about what they think of you. If there is one skill in life that will benefit you more, then I do not know of it.

Like so many other moments of psychological balance, the weighting between caring and not caring is crucial. No one wants to be the sort of person who doesn't care about things. Because that person is dead behind the eyes. But if you care so much about external factors – and, especially, about the opinions of others – then you are lost. This is the real key to knowing how to talk about yourself in front of other people and how to portray yourself on social media. If you genuinely feel you have no idea how you want to present yourself to others and you are lost, then it's time to go on a journey of self-discovery, whether it's through reading a lot of books, listening to a lot of podcasts or asking some of your friends what they value in you as a person.

When I hear women worrying about how they are portraying themselves on social media, or about how they really wanted to tell someone at a party that they had just got a new job but they didn't in case they looked as if they were showing off, or about how they'd really like to take credit for their team's deal but Tim actually did the bulk of the work and he's better at talking about it . . . Well, I just want to tear my hair out. It's part self-consciousness, part self-esteem. And the stronger your self-esteem, the less conscious you feel about yourself and the more you are able to stop thinking about yourself all the time and focus on other people.

How to self-promote in real life without being a complete asshole

The business of the school reunion, meetings with friends you haven't seen for ages, catch-up sessions with old colleagues and meeting people you don't know at parties or networking events all comes under the same banner: this is about releasing your self-talk into the wild. So you are going to have to find the words to say out loud things you might only say to yourself in private. For those of us who struggle with articulating anything good that we have achieved, even to ourselves, this is a big challenge. There are a lot of reasons why you might have started finding it difficult to think or talk positively or even factually about yourself. Or perhaps you feel as if you've always been like this.

There are good excuses for this reticence. You're scared of sounding boastful. You're scared of intimidating the other person. You don't want to attract envy or scorn. You can remember hearing comments like these when you were a child: 'What makes you so special?' 'Who cares?' 'So what? No one is impressed.' 'Big deal. There are loads of things you can't do.' 'No one likes a show-off.'

Where does this stuff come from? Some of it is misogyny. ('Know your place, little woman.') Some of it is a sort of puritanism. Some of it is class discrimination, which is another way of saying: 'Know your place in the scheme of things.' It's all a way of saying that any thoughts of self-betterment and thinking positive things about yourself are a waste of time because, ultimately, nothing is really going to work out for you so it would be better if you just gave up on everything. No one can possibly think that this is a good way to live.

These thoughts and habits are not gendered but I would be surprised if they weren't more common in women. I don't say that from a place of judgement, as I'm intimate with these thoughts myself. There can be a huge contradiction between the things you are told as a child are supposedly possible for you and what is actually possible for you. If anything, this disconnect has worsened and become more confusing in the twenty-first century. Girls are told that they can be and do everything. Yet there is still a pay gap. Boys are told that they have had it good for too long and it's time to make way for the girls, and yet girls' exam results and university entries have been outstripping those of boys for some time.

I'm not sure how we unpick all this at a societal level. Clearly, politics, policy, law and structural change make all the difference. But the situation is definitely going to persist if we don't unpick it at an individual level. So we need to start where it's easy and possible to start: with ourselves. This means talking to yourself in a way that reminds you of your achievements. It means learning to state factually, in a relaxed and comfortable way, who you are and what you do. I have lost count of the number of women (yes, I'm sorry but it is usually women) who I have met at events who downplay what they do, make it sound less important or who apologize for it. Don't even get me started on women introducing themselves at events. Women have a tendency to give

only their first name, even when introducing themselves on a public platform. I have never seen a man do
this. We need to know your full name. We need to hear
your job title and what you do without you apologizing
for it or suggesting that it's not a big deal (it is) or that
you don't really do that job (you do). It can feel embar-
rassing to state your first name and surname and say
what you do, but the more you do it, the more natural
it becomes. The more you say, 'Er, I'm Sarah and, er,
well, I don't really do anything that important . . .' the
more you put yourself down.

There are, of course, ways of going too far in the
opposite direction, which are not to be recommended.
I once met a man who was CEO of a big company. I
didn't know his job when I met him: I knew he did
something interesting as we were meeting at a corporate event and he was unlikely to be there unless he did
something interesting. But when I asked him what he
did, he replied, 'I dream big dreams.' I tried to hide the
fact that I was gritting my teeth already and said, 'Yes,
but what's your job?' He replied, as if he were a Bud-
dhist monk, 'If the bins need emptying in my office, I
empty the bins.' I knew immediately that he was the
CEO of a major enterprise and an extremely annoying
person. I also immediately suspected that he had
never actually emptied the bins.

There is a middle path between saying, 'Oh, I'm no
one, really' and saying something idiotically grandiose

like 'I create the canvas for others to drawn upon.' It begins with this business of learning to say your name in full, simply and clearly. This sounds really obvious but I know from having worked with hundreds of women in my workshops that when they are asked to introduce themselves to a large group of people, even in a low-pressure setting, many of them will struggle to say their name (and surname) in full along with their job title. They will mumble part of it and throw away the rest: 'Er, I'm Kate? And I work in HR?' The question mark denotes 'uptalk', when we send our voice up at the end of a sentence. See if you can hear the difference in your head: 'My name is Kate Watson. And I'm a human resources manager.' This exercise is really important to master. Because if you cannot say your name properly and confidently and you cannot say your job title without cringing, then I really do question whether you are using your one precious life in the way that you could be using it. It's a great exercise for figuring out whether you're OK with who you are. And maybe a sense of self is what a lot of this is really about. Are you OK with who you are? If so, be it and say it. If you're not, then change something. This sounds easy. But it is the work of a lifetime to be at ease with yourself. Being able to state your name and what you do is the tiniest part of it.

Mastering this bit is 90 per cent of the 'Who do you think you are?' challenge. If you can learn to say in a straightforward and easygoing way that this is who you are and this is what you do, then you will suddenly find yourself being able to say other things much more easily. To be straight with friends and strangers about what is going on with your work, good and bad. To be factual about the good bits, proud where it's appropriate and honest about the tricky bits.

Once you've got that down, it's important to start acknowledging your achievements. Let's be honest, no one really cares about them apart from you so you might as well learn to state them in a matter-of-fact way. It's worth thinking about why you're embarrassed or feel weird about saying stuff about your work. This is an important thing to nail because, otherwise, you find yourself either downplaying your achievements in a way that is false and, to a large extent, depressing, or you end up being generally negative about things to the point of being self-negating.

A lot of the difficulty is to do with jargon and the ridiculous words we use in work. I became very conscious of this whilst working as a journalist as I would frequently interview people who would say things that were clearly normal in their line of work but that actually meant nothing at all. (Such as: 'My role is to manage stakeholder outcomes as part of our verticals.' I still have no idea what this means but people in jobs where you have to wear a lanyard say things like this all the time.) I would find myself thinking – and sometimes saying out loud – 'Yes, but what does that actually mean?' I have been in situations where I've been asked to advise a CEO on how to talk in a media interview and the first question I will ask is, 'How would you describe what your job is to a five-year-old child?' That is not to say that the audience you're addressing are like five-year-old children and you need to patronize and talk down to them. It's the opposite: you are treating people as adults by paying them the courtesy of clarity. If you can make what you do sound clear to a five-year-old, then you can talk about it in an engaging and straightforward way with absolutely anyone. For the moments where you might have to be clear about who you are and what you do – in a job interview, at a reunion, on stage, as part of a panel, at a party – practise saying what you would say if a child asked you, 'What's the best thing that has happened in your job recently?' And imagine what you would say if someone asked you, 'Yes, but what do you actually do?'

CLIMB

● Maintaining a healthy attitude towards self-promotion is key. Be aware that how comfortable you feel about it will change at different times in your life: sometimes you might feel more confident about putting yourself out there than at other times. This is normal. One incredibly helpful thing to do: appoint a circle of close friends or current or former colleagues whose job it is to tell you when you have gone too far (by posting too frequently or too openly on social media, for example). It is so important to choose the right people. Do not choose someone who is incredibly shy and embarrassed to be alive. And do not choose someone whose idea of being self-deprecating is to limit themselves to ten Facebook posts a day. It's a balance, it's subjective and it's up to you. But it's good to have the opinion of people who are in your corner. (Make sure they are in your corner.)

● People like to celebrate success and they like to be associated with people who are successful. This might not be humanity's greatest achievement but it's simply a fact. If something happens to you that can be counted as a 'win' – a launch, a celebration, an award, a prize, an anniversary, good news of almost any kind – then you have a free pass to put it on social media. Or let it be the first thing you mention in a conversation.

('I'm celebrating because I've just been nominated for Employee of the Week!') Only really miserable people will begrudge you this.

● The things that fall into a grey area when it comes to self-promotion are the things that cannot be counted as news or a celebration. This is where we can all stray into over-taxing other people's attention and generosity. You have to decide where you stand. Are you going to be modest or brazen? I think you need to have experienced both extremes to know which is best. Sometimes we have to be brazen and know what it feels like to promote ourselves a bit too much. Sometimes we have to be too modest to realize that, actually, we're just hiding away. Experiment. That way we know where the happy medium lies. That place is different for everyone.

● Whatever you can put out into the world that counts as sharing expertise, revealing knowledge, passing on advice or giving recommendations is rarely taxing on people's attention. If you feel uncomfortable about self-promotion, instead of saying, 'Look at what I'm doing,' say, 'This is what I've learned,' or 'This is what I wish I'd known.'

LIFT

● If you are intensely terrified of self-promotion and just cannot bear it, congratulate yourself: you can be

one of the people in this world who devotes themselves to promoting others. Just make sure you cast
your net far and wide (because no one wants to hear
about your same two over-achieving friends over and
over again).

● If you are OK with spontaneity and ad hoc communication, just share other people's achievements as and
when. If you feel as if you need a bit more structure, set
yourself a target: share five book recommendations
every week or post a 'Role Model of the Week'. Regu-
larity and consistency are great, easy ways to create
content, so force yourself to do a post promoting
another woman every Monday at 9 a.m. because it's
just what you do then.

● If you are good at social media and have a relaxed
attitude towards self-promotion (or you've learned
how to acquire one), think about how you could teach
it to other women who might want to know how to be
that way. Talk about it on Instagram Stories or Facebook Live. Offer to do a workshop for your colleagues,
give tips and lead a discussion about the pitfalls. If you
see a woman hiding her light under a bushel on social
media, talk to her about why that it is. (She may have
very sensible reasons. Or a life. Or it may be that she
needs some encouragement from someone who can
reassure her that it doesn't look as if she's showing off
if she writes a blog post every week.)

● If you have the opportunity to interview, quote, mention or highlight another woman or her work, do it. If you get offered a speaking opportunity or a conference place that you can't take up, put some other women's names forward.

3

How to Network and Meet Other People (without Wanting to Hide under a Table)

'You are who you surround yourself with.'
Selena Gomez

In the film *When Harry Met Sally*, there is a series of cameos by supposedly real-life couples about how they met. They are the sort of adorable old couples who have been together for over fifty years and they talk to camera about the secret of longevity in a marriage. I say 'supposedly' because the original idea was that this would be documentary footage of real case studies. But when they tried to film couples talking about how they met they took ages to tell their stories and their accounts didn't match up. They ended up scripting everything and re-filming it using actors. One of the couples talks about how, as teenagers, their eyes met across a crowded room. The woman remembers how surprised she was when she realized that this boy was coming to talk to her. She thought he was headed over to talk to her friend Maxine. Then she says something very telling about the stereotype we have of people who are charismatic, attractive and make friends easily: 'People were always crossing rooms to talk to Maxine.' This, in a nut-shell, is the myth we have about networking: we think that we have to be Maxine. And that if we're not, there's just no point bothering.

The expression 'networking' is hateful. But all it means is 'meeting other people'. The pain, stress and anxiety around formal 'networking' and all the questions it throws up are unbearable: 'Does this person expect something from me? Am I supposed to help them? How do I ask them to help me? Am I interesting enough? Am I too junior to talk to them? How do I open the conversation?' All these anxieties are excruciating, even for women meeting other women.

I hesitate even to use the word 'networking'. Used in a formal sense, it is the worst kind of commodification of the natural human urge to talk to other people and get to know them. It suggests subverting this innocent urge into something self-serving: to mine the people around you for information, contacts and personal benefit. Not only is this a horrible thing to do but it's a horrible thing for anyone to think of you doing. If, during a conversation with someone, you start to think, 'Oh no, this person is networking with me . . .', it's worse than thinking, 'This person is going to kill me.' Because at least you are justified in running away from someone who wants to kill you. Trapped in the corner of a room with a person who's networking you, it can feel as though there's no escape.

Let us assume that no one really wants to network. All any of us really wants is an easier life and to achieve our goals (the most important of which might be to have an easier life). All we really want is to feel a bit more comfortable around other people and less self-conscious. This is, I think, the key to 'networking'. (And let's keep those inverted commas there for a bit in case you think I am someone who would ever use the word 'networking' without underlining it as a ridiculous concept.) We are afraid sometimes even to meet other people in case they think that we are 'networking' with them. This fear, even in situations where it's not likely, is so paralysing that it makes people insanely uncomfortable at parties, when they should just be having a good time.

There are loads of easy tricks using body language and conversational gambits that make these conversations easy. But it's also important to switch your mindset: focus on the other person instead of being self-obsessed. Stop making it about yourself and think about the other people who are there. Think about what you could (easily) do for them, without overreaching. If there isn't anything you can do for them, then just be someone light-hearted and easygoing for them to talk to about themselves for five minutes.

I once interviewed the historian Margaret McMillan and she talked about a brilliant tip her mother had given her when she was a shy young girl: 'Be a good guest.' If you are at a party or a work event or a conference or anywhere, think, 'What can I do to be a good guest?' This does not literally mean that you need to take care of the catering arrangements or start collecting everyone's coats. Although in some situations those could be useful decisions and I have done these things at parties many times. But it does mean using your imagination to think, 'What does this event need? What do these people need?' In some situations it might need someone who listens and pays court and acts as an audience for people with big egos. At other times, it might need someone to inject a bit of life and soul into the party by raising a toast to the host or by encouraging others towards the buffet or the dance floor. It could mean realizing that you are one of the people at the party who knows quite a few of the guests there and can help out by making introductions.

That's it. Simple. And yet it's not so simple for many of us. Few people like to take responsibility in these situations. They worry that they might introduce two guests who don't like each other and that they will be blamed for the introduction. They worry that others will think, 'Who is she to raise a toast? Who asked her to do that?' They worry that people will think they are boring so perhaps they had better not impose themselves on anyone. To all this, I say: back up. When you are thinking that you do not deserve to be alive, that you don't deserve to take up space at this party/conference/event, you need to back up. Of course you deserve to be there. And you deserve to do whatever you feel like doing, providing it doesn't involve running away and hiding. To think otherwise is to insult the person who invited you. They are not an idiot. They invited you because they wanted you to be there and to participate.

In the end I think many people are not scared of 'networking' or 'social gatherings'. What they are afraid of is taking responsibility and being held to account. And they are afraid of being judged. What makes you think you can just come up and introduce yourself to him? What makes you think you are interesting enough to talk to her? What if you say something excruciating or inappropriate to them? Perhaps it would be better to go and hide by the vol-au-vents and leave after half an hour.

It's acceptable to feel this way if you're an awkward teenager. It would be weird if you didn't. But if you are an adult, you don't really have any excuse. There will be people at this party who have had a harder time in life than you have. (There always is, in every room.) There will be people who are having a tough day. There will be people who want to be there even less than you do. What can you do to make this event more bearable for them? All you have to do is smile, listen, ask basic questions: 'What brings you here?' 'Do you know anyone here?' 'How was your day?' The questions can even be a bit negative or suggestive: 'Do you like these kinds of events?' 'Got any tips for getting through events like this?' 'I get nervous at these events. Do you mind if I talk to you?' No one will be anything but intensely relieved if you say these things to them.

Of course, there are always horrible people at parties who look at you as if you are a three-headed alien for daring to talk to them. And other people who are utterly charming and all sweetness and light but who look directly beyond your shoulder for the entire conversation. Personally, I always seem to come across people who stare directly at my collarbone or the top of my chest for the duration of an interaction, making me think that I have either a massive wart growing there or a stain on my clothing. Whenever this happens to me, I try to check in discreetly with others and usually they will say something like, 'Oh, yes, Carol always does that. She's a bit short-sighted.' Yet again, more evidence that it is very rarely you who has the problem. Except for the one time when I really did have a massive patch of baby sick down a silk blouse and no one told me until the end of the evening.

Networking for a purpose

The inverted commas have come off, now that we're into the thick of it. It's time to admit that sometimes we do network consciously and for a purpose. I'd be lying if I said I had never done this, although I would not have used that language or that thought process. ('The work contact I really want to make is here! Let me go and network with her whilst wearing my best networking smile!') We all have things that we need and things that we want to happen. If we are ambitious in our work (and I hope that we are), then we will have things that we want to bring to fruition. I don't believe in attending parties or events exclusively for reasons of self-interest. You should leave a lot of room for fun and serendipity. But sometimes you do need to approach a certain person for a certain reason and some people would insist on calling that networking. Don't think of it that way if you want to sleep at night. Instead think of it straightforwardly as 'picking your moment' or 'making the most of an opportunity' or 'fate'.

If you are at an event and you see someone who you would not otherwise have the opportunity to meet and it is someone you would like to get to know better, possibly to ask them to do something, or to ask their advice about something, then you should approach them. Could you be rebuffed in this situation? Yes. Could you succeed in making life-long friends with someone who was previously a stranger? Yes. Could you get what you want from them? Sometimes yes. Sometimes no. Sometimes you might get something completely different.

You do have to know how to behave in these situations and whether what you want is appropriate. If I see

Madonna at an event, for example, can I go up and say, 'Hi, Madonna, would you come on my podcast?' In theory, I can and it might be worth doing to get a story out of it. However, this approach is unlikely to work. Instead you want to be strategic. Find out who she is with. She is unlikely to be there on her own. She will be with a PR person or an assistant. That is the person you need to talk to and engage. That is the person you need to tell about your podcast request and ask their honest opinion. Is it something she'd be interested in? What's the best way to approach her? If they like you, they may even introduce you. If they're wary, at least you might get their email and you can follow up. If you are thinking, 'All I want to do is meet Madonna and get a selfie,' then that's OK but that's a completely different goal. Then you just have to have the guts to reveal yourself as a crazy fan and expect to be treated as a crazy fan: if she's in the mood to indulge you, she will. If she isn't, she won't. (I should be clear here that I have never been at an event with Madonna and am not sure how cool I'd be about it. If any situation would be likely to lead to a restraining order, it would be this one.)

The same goes for people you might want to meet for work reasons, because you're job hunting or there's someone who can help you with a project. If you can manage a chance encounter, great. If you can speak straightforwardly and honestly about what you're looking for help with, great. If you can't, then have an open and warm conversation and try to make a good-to-neutral impression and follow up with an email. The golden rule is to not waste people's time. Bumbling on about your nerves or how busy they must be and how could they possibly make time for you and probably your request is foolish anyway . . . Let's dispense with the craven self-deprecation. All this is wasting someone's time and is just you indulging your ego. Get in there. Be friendly. Assume the other person is having a bad day. Be straightforward. Then get the hell out.

This rule goes doubly for networking by email. If you want chapter and verse on how to get people you don't know to reply to your emails, I suggest reading Alex Banayan's *The Third Door: The Wild Quest to Uncover How the World's Most Successful People Launched Their Careers*. (In a nutshell: a successful email campaign as part of a job search or a major ask relies on you finding the difference between demonstrating commitment and being a hassle.) The entrepreneur Tim Ferriss has talked a lot about the importance of sending emails that are no longer than five sentences long. You need a clear ask that says in as few words as possible why you are sending this email. You need to define the parameters: 'A response of two lines would be great.' And Ferriss explains that you need to let the person off the hook: 'I know you're busy so if you don't have time to respond, I totally understand.' (Personally, most of the time I wouldn't bother with this disclaimer. The person doesn't care whether you understand or not. Either they want to reply to your email or they don't.)

I have learned this the hard way over the years, asking people to take part in literary festivals, comedy shows, podcasts, radio documentaries and print articles. Be succinct and transparent. Give them an easy 'out'. If they really don't want to do it, it's better to know early than to chase them with no answer for a long time only to realize that their silence means 'No'. I still frequently make mistakes and send emails that are too long or too begging. These emails never work. Sometimes, though, it's just because your timing is off. You can't predict that. And that is also true face to face. Introduce yourself to someone at a party at the wrong time and if you've just interrupted a conversation that was important to them . . . Well, you've lost. Meet them when they were desperate to escape someone . . . Then you win. But those moments are not things that you can know. You have to be willing to take a risk. In order to get comfortable with networking and in order for your networking to bear any fruit, you need to be able to handle being bad at networking and it not yielding results. This is a big problem with networking: we would be happy to do it if we could guarantee success and getting what we want. In reality it's a huge gamble.

Is your women's network a waste of time?

This is a clickbait question which Katie Hopkins or Piers Morgan could have written. But I ask it without malice or bias. When I say 'women's network' I am talking about an organized group who come together in support, whether it's part of a company, an association or a slightly more informal version of a members' club. Many women spend time networking with each other, trying to support each other, recruiting 'allies', attempting to get men to come to the women's networking events, and I would like to think that this is not all a waste of time. So how do you make 'women's networks' meaningful? It's not good enough to say: 'Form a women's network!' If that network is going to have a point, you have to acknowledge the potential pitfalls and drawbacks and work hard to avoid them. This is another problem people have with networking: they think it is going to be easier to do it in a group where everyone has agreed in advance that the purpose of the group is . . . to network. Newsflash: this does not make it easier. If anything, the transparency of the networking makes it more awkward.

These groups can inadvertently end up being more divisive than inclusive. While working with one particular company I heard that behind closed doors male colleagues were calling the women's network 'the suffragettes'. This is not the first time I've heard of this kind of belittling of a women's network, so it didn't surprise me. But it did give me pause. Sometimes we're simply not aware of the scale of what we're up against. The idea of equality is still derided in many quarters in the way that it was when women were chaining themselves to the railings of Downing Street over a hundred years ago. And sometimes these views rush to the surface again as a result of even the most modest of women's networking initiatives.

Am I saying it's not worth starting a women's group? No. It can be an important symbol of support, a talking shop and a place to experiment with ideas and solutions. It is incredibly difficult to make progress on the issue of equality at work when, first, not everyone agrees that there is a problem and, second, not everyone agrees how to fix it. There is still an issue with convincing those for whom this is not a personal problem (i.e. men who have had ample opportunity for promotion). Psychologically it is very difficult to persuade people that the power they have has not entirely been earned by them, that some of that power might have been bestowed upon them by bias. And even if they do acknowledge that patriarchal good fortune, it's not a given that they'll want to pass some of the power back over. But unless we can make people see what is going on, we are not going to make progress with the issue of inequality.

Sometimes it's as if we're in the middle of a sea

of voices which are drowning each other out. First you have the old-school types, the ones who call the women's network 'the suffragettes' and who are also horrified at the behaviour of 'snowflakes'. These are the people who want to believe that they've got where they have because of 'meritocracy' and are not interested in 'checking their privilege'. They are blind to any information or statistics or arguments that suggest that there is something wrong with the status quo. As far as they are concerned, the status quo is working out just fine. The only thing wrong with it are your complaints about how it's not working out for you. So perhaps you could shut up a bit?

Then you've got the new thinkers born in the digital age who are utterly mortified by the idea that anyone should resist checking their privilege. They see injustice and they want action now. They are not interested in all the excuses and explanations and the reasons behind the injustice. I'm familiar with this way of thinking from working with people much younger than me. (Starting with younger comedians who first forced me to engage with Facebook over ten years ago when I was starting out in stand-up. I thought they were idiotic and that social media was never going to take off. Go figure.) I see it even more strongly in my children, who are in their mid teens. They are ridiculously politically correct and alive to inequality. And quite right too. But they are going to get a massive shock when they get out into the real world and come up against people who not only don't care about equality but actively want to stamp it out. Those people aren't going anywhere.

And in the middle you have people like me who probably wouldn't have noticed fifteen years ago if a conference panel was all-male or all-white (I know – I'm embarrassed to write this but it's true). We are the ones who now realize how slowly diversity and inclusion are moving forward. The people in the middle recognize that the older dinosaurs don't want an answer and the younger, digital generation doesn't really have a workable answer (especially because the dinosaurs are still in charge). It's up to people in the middle to find a way to get the two extremes talking to each other and seeing things from each other's point of view. Because the dinosaurs are not going away (and with recent developments in medicine and the need to work longer and later they will probably be around for at least another thirty or forty years) and the digital generation is not going to shut up. Something's got to give.

There is an interesting contradiction between the way we go about asking for change and trying to prove that equality is a good idea for us all. The former tech CEO turned author, keynote speaker and TED talker Margaret Heffernan argues that no advocacy is successful when you advocate for yourself. People think you are just saying, 'Women should get more pay' because you yourself want to receive more pay. (You can see her logic here.) In her view, you should only advocate for groups of which you are not a member. This makes perfect sense but it's hard to make it play out in practice. Ideally, we would all be the sort of person who wants to fix things for other people. In reality, we are much better at pushing really hard to get them fixed for ourselves.

So how can we make these things look less selfish? Clearly we are not recruiting enough people to the inequality cause fast enough. We need to recruit individuals who don't directly benefit – including those who fear that they might actually have to give up power. Because it's not true that women are doing this just for themselves. We want to fix it for others and so that no one has to argue for this all over again in the future. The short-term gains might be 'selfish'. But the long-term gains are entirely selfless. How to enlist more people who won't benefit in the short-term? Perhaps if a hundred years ago the battles of the suffragettes had been won by people who weren't suffragettes or, indeed, women, but by people who already had the vote and cared so much about equality that they were willing to advocate for those without the vote . . . Well, perhaps women's groups would not now be called 'suffragettes' as a derogatory, dismissive term. And perhaps women's groups wouldn't have to exist.

I am reminded here – and awed – by the example of

the BBC journalist Carrie Gracie, who won her case against her employer when she found out that she was being paid less than male colleagues at the same level. As part of her case she was awarded £361,000 in back pay. (Think of the cheque! It's mind-blowing!) What she did next is an extreme way of proving that her case was not for herself but for everyone: she donated every single penny of the money that she was owed to the Equal Pay Advice Service and the Fawcett Society – the UK's leading charity campaigning for gender equality. She gave it all away, even though it was owed to her and even though her male colleagues had received that money as part of their salary without even thinking about it.

I don't suggest that when any of us successfully claims back money that is owed to us we say, 'Thanks for that money – I'm now going to donate it to a women's refuge.' (Although please take a photo of the look on your boss's face if you do this and send it to me.) But Carrie Gracie's case symbolizes something worth thinking about. How do we make networking and these demands for change inclusive and not selfish? How do we make sure we signal that we are doing this for the good of everyone and not just for the good of ourselves as individuals? How do we embody this idea of lifting as we climb in our actions? These are huge questions and the answers to them will be different for everyone. But I've suggested some in the following exercises.

CLIMB

● Take responsibility for building your own network. Don't expect someone to do it for you. Some women think there is a 'network' waiting out there for them to join and this network will provide instant friends, contacts and mentors without them having to do anything. They imagine other people have this and envy them. This just isn't true. Our 'networks' exist in our own heads and are not transferable. No one is attending some amazing party that you are never invited to. (Yes, this is a metaphor for life.)

● Gretchen Rubin, author of *Better than Before: Mastering the Habits of Our Everyday Lives*, has a great piece of advice about making new friends: decide you will make three new friends in the next six months. Start looking out for who those three people will be – they quickly present themselves. It's a manageable goal. Try something similar with networking. Pinpoint three people you want to get to know over the next six months. If they would also benefit from knowing each other, make it your goal to get the four of you together at the end of the six months. (Maybe don't tell people you did this. It feels a bit like stalking. Your secret is safe with me.)

● Think long-term and not immediate gain. There is no point in networking with someone at a party, getting their email and doing nothing with it. Similarly, there is no point in meeting that person for coffee once and never seeing them again. Real, meaningful networking is a relationship: you have things in common, you look out for each other, there's a connection. It is not about ticking a box so that you can post on LinkedIn.

● Be gracious if someone tries to help you network or makes a connection on your behalf and it doesn't work out. Sometimes these things aren't meant to be. Be grateful that they tried. Appreciate attempts and gestures rather than being focused on the outcome. Always say: 'Thanks for trying to make that happen.' We network in hope. It doesn't always turn out as we'd have liked. We need to remember to say thank you anyway.

● Networking is a hopeful and sometimes targeted activity. We do it for a reason. That can be burdensome for everyone. Take some of the transactional quality out of it by networking with people who have seemingly nothing to do with anything you're focused on but who you just find interesting. That can lead to unusual things.

LIFT

● Give status to others whenever you can. Introduce people to each other (face to face and digitally), especially when one of them might be afraid to approach the other. Don't be controlling about the introductions you make: whether they hit it off or not is not your responsibility. Be the spark. The fire – or lack thereof – is not your problem.

● If there are opportunities to which you have to say no (to a party, a meeting, a conference, a speaking invitation), offer to make a connection with someone in your network who might benefit. No need to be controlling: it works out or it doesn't. We all love to know that someone thought of us, even if it eventually didn't work out. (Please do think of me if you can't take up that all-expenses-paid conference invitation to Bali.)

● If you're part of a networking group or you are set-ting one up, think about how that group can make inclusion and diversity part of the biggest conversa-tion possible. This is not just about fixing things for women, it's about making sure that all the inherent biases of past centuries are not repeated. So if you host events, yes, of course, put women front and centre. But have someone introduce the event who is not from your group. Have someone give a vote of thanks who is not naturally one of your supporters – or who represents another cause entirely. This is not about 'virtue-signalling' or being seen to do these things. It's about genuinely trying to find a way through the prob-lems we're all facing.

● Encourage connections that work for life, not just for work. Introduce people because you think they will enjoy each other's company and make each other laugh – and not necessarily be remotely useful to each other in a professional sense. This might be the most useful thing any of us ever does in our lives: introduce people to other people who make them feel good.

4

How to Make Sure You
(and Other Women)
Get Paid What You Deserve

'Each time a woman stands up for herself, without knowing it possibly, without claiming it, she stands up for all women.'
Maya Angelou

One of the most challenging moments of my early career was when I had a staff job on a newspaper as a writer and I found out a male colleague who was doing a lot less work than me was being paid almost double what I was being paid. When I brought this up with my editor, I was told that I seemed to have a large shoe collection, so what was I complaining about? This was an annoying thing to hear. The fact of the salary mis-match was bad enough. But it was made worse by the fact that I was being unnecessarily over-diligent and swotty in my work at the time. (Note to others: Don't do this.) My male colleague, as you will have already guessed, was unnecessarily lazy and unproductive, producing around one article to my ten. At the time, I thought his attitude was idiotic. Looking back, I realize that he was extremely sensible and shrewd and it was

I who was being the idiot. His move (or, really, complete lack of moves, as he mostly sat at his desk inert, listening to music on his headphones) was genius, as he made his work seem more special and important because there was less of it. When he handed work in, people were impressed and excited because he had done something. When I handed work in, no one noticed, as it was just another product rolling off the Groskop conveyor belt of miracles. You could have set your watch by my pointless and thankless overworking.

The point was, though, that we were supposed to be equals in terms of status and salary. So I saw red. Furthermore, my shoe collection was really not that large and at the time I would have found it completely shocking to spend more than £50 on a pair of shoes. Most of my shoes were from Zara or Debenhams' sale. I was particularly fond of the Debenhams Blue Cross sale at this juncture in my life. And here I am, even now, defending myself and trying to prove that my shoes were not that expensive when the point is this: it is not your boss's business what you spend your money on. The shoe comment was the world's most patronizing red herring.

At the time, I was about to get married and get a mortgage. Although that's also not exactly relevant either, as I hate hearing those stories where single women get turned down for a pay rise because 'Brian's wife doesn't work and they've just had twins and bought a second home in the Dordogne.' What I mean is that in my own mind I was thinking: 'Mate, I am taking on adult responsibilities here. Don't pay me like a child. Even if it is a child in fabulous navy-satin kitten heels. A colleague who is supposed to be at the same level as me does way less work and is being paid £15,000 more than I am. Doesn't that bother you?' I was gutted and did not know where to turn. I knew I would not be able to prove that my colleague was doing less work than me. I knew that I could hardly convince my boss that if he paid me more I would do even more work because I was already doing a lot of work and this would have been physically impossible. The conveyor belt of miracles was already working at full capacity. Instead I took the only option that was open to me: subterfuge.

When we talk about money and work – which is often – the thing we don't talk about is that, in most jobs, it's really difficult to 'get legal on their ass'. (This is a technical term.) Of course, sometimes legal action is justified, necessary and, frankly, the only realistic option. Often, though, it's not even a consideration. When you realize that you're being paid less than a male colleague doing the same job, taking the case to a lawyer feels like launching a bomb, when all you probably want to do is stick a paperclip in your boss's eyes (gently) to make them do the right thing. When it happened to me, I got around it the old-fashioned way: by getting a job offer from a place where I didn't want to work but would have been prepared to if I had to. This took me several phone calls, some meetings and was a process that lasted about a month. Ultimately, it was good research as well as a good move: I realized that I was capable of representing what I did to other people and I got to find out how much more money someone else in another company was willing to pay for my work. I also worked out that the person who was able to give me this extra money in my current job was not my editor but the managing editor, who controlled the budget. I made an appointment to see her, explained that I had a job offer and the salary they were willing to pay me. I said I didn't want to leave but that financially I had no choice. 'Leave it with me,' she said. And I didn't even have to mention my colleague, who continued his inertia as before.

Interestingly – and this is another one of those little things that we don't talk about – that pay rise was worth a lot more to me than I knew at the time, as a few months later I took redundancy. And the redundancy payment was based on salary. It turned out there was a lot more at stake than the simple fact of my monthly salary and the disparity with a male colleague's. But, looking back, what this episode taught me more than anything was that trying to do things on your own is intensely, er, lonely. Here I was, desperately trying to climb. And the only lift I could get was from myself. That was better than nothing, of course. And I'm glad I found a way through. But if I had had a senior colleague who could have seen that situation and helped me through it – maybe even before I had found out about the salary disparity – it would have completely transformed my attitude towards that workplace.

Instead I learned a lesson which is partially helpful but also limiting and slightly sad: 'If you want to get anything done around here, you'll have to do it yourself.' With hindsight, I can see that I helped myself but I did nothing to challenge the status quo. Someone else probably faced the same battle a year later. There is no perfect way to behave and we can only do our best with the knowledge that we have at the time. But if I had thought a bit more about lifting and less about climbing then I might have found the courage to ask for someone else's help – and that, in turn, might have influenced the culture.

Don't ask, don't get

Whilst financial success may not be everyone's definition of ambition, an obvious goal in climbing is making sure you're being paid what you deserve. This, in its own way, is another way to lift: advocate for your own worth in order to underline the importance of all women being paid what they're worth. The more we see women speaking openly and straightforwardly about money, the easier it is for all of us. One of the biggest barriers holding women back from getting more money on an individual level is the ability to articulate and define what we want and then to ask for it. I know a lot of people will be reading this and thinking, 'What about collective action? What about organizational change? Women should not have to face this on an individual level.' And that is absolutely right. We should all join our unions. We should all stay informed and support mass moves towards equal pay. But I know from many different women in different industries that this workplace stuff plays out in com- plicated and nuanced ways. Often it's down to an individual relationship with a particular person. It can be to do with timing. It can be to do with the culture of the company you work in. This is not to say that we shouldn't fight for universal standards. A lot of the equal pay reporting in recent years has been ground- breaking, making gender-pay-gap statistics public so that we can compare companies. This is what drives long-term change and this work is essential. But it does not help you to go into the office tomorrow (or this afternoon, let's not hang about) and ask for another 5 per cent.

So much of the pay issue is about entitlement, which is just one of the ways in which we can hold ourselves back. The old chestnut of feeling 'not good enough' or 'undeserving' comes up regularly in my encounters with women. Women don't apply for jobs unless they think they meet at least 80 per cent of the job requirements. The data says that men will apply if they meet 20 per cent. American professor of psychology Art Markman revealed in the *Harvard Business Review* that he told his own son: 'If you're completely qualified for the job you applied for, you're aiming too low.' We need to make sure we tell this to our daughters and to ourselves.

The 'massive bastard' technique

We are all driven towards wanting to feel comfortable, avoid judgement and not risk having other people think that we are awful. Tara Mohr, the author of *Playing Big: A Practical Guide for Brilliant Women Like You*, calls this 'the invisible drive that shapes our lives, often unconsciously'. (Please don't be put off by the subtitle of that book. It's the absolute bible for overcoming your limitations.) Mohr describes this as the drive to avoid discomfort, to stay away from the risk of being disliked or thought of as pushy or arrogant. It is what happens, says Mohr, when we think to ourselves: 'There is something I don't want to feel.' You don't want to feel greedy so you don't ask for a pay rise. You don't want to feel patronizing so you don't offer advice to a younger colleague. You don't want to look competitive so you don't apply for a post your friend has applied for. Mohr's answer is to think yourself into the uncomfortable: imagine what it would be like if you felt the thing but you did it anyway. I call it the 'massive bastard' technique. What would you do if you didn't mind anyone thinking you were a massive bastard? What would an actual massive bastard do in this situation? And why aren't you doing it?

Apologies to any sensitive readers for the language here but it's important because it represents an extremity. It can't just be a 'mean person' or 'an unpleasant colleague' or 'a bit of a git'. It has to be the nuclear option: the massive bastard. It's very effective to pursue this line of thought. If there is something you want to do (like ask for more money because you know a project is worth more money, propose a big idea, recommend yourself for a role without waiting to be 'chosen') but you don't want the feelings that go with it, you can think to yourself: 'What would the massive bastard do?'

This is extreme and it matters that it shocks you – at least a bit. It's a way of shaking yourself out of timid behaviour and it encourages you to develop the mindset of someone who is possibly a bit unhinged, definitely someone who ruthlessly goes after what they want. Instead of being someone who doesn't ask for enough – or is too scared to ask for anything at all – you need to think about what someone would ask for if they were completely deranged, arrogant and self-centred.

Let's say you're going after a piece of work for which

you have been offered £500 but you know someone else has been paid £800 to do it. Let's assume you're not keen to do the work for £500, firstly because you know you don't have enough time to do it for that price, and, secondly, because you know someone else was paid more. You have grounds to ask for more. You know that you need to ask for £1,000 in order to get the £800. That's just a fact of negotiation. At the very least, you will perhaps by offered £600, which is a 20 per cent increase on the original offer and better than a kick in the teeth. The employer might say, 'No. We only have £500.' Or, perhaps even worse, they might get offended and say, 'Sorry, we went with someone else in the end.' (Newsflash: this can happen at any time anyway and there's nothing you can do about it. Unless you move to a contract, of course, where you know exactly what you're being paid.)

While you're running through all these scenarios in your mind, you can also think, 'What would a massive bastard do?' A massive bastard might say, '£500? Are you joking? I would only do this for £50,000 and I would also need to have use of a private jet for a week. And I expect you to give me a wardrobe allowance of £10,000. Oh, yes, and this needs to go to contract within twenty-four hours or I can't do it at all.'

You are not going to do that because you are not a massive bastard. Neither am I. Most of the time, anyway. But what this extreme example gives you is a bit of space in your brain. And it gives you some levity and fun in a negotiation. It makes it into something entertaining and to be taken lightly rather than another opportunity to punish yourself. Instead of thinking to yourself, 'You're lucky to be offered any work in the first place, just take the £500,' you can think, 'They're very lucky that I'm not asking for the private-jet option.'

You can also water down the 'bastard' idea and be realistic about it. What would someone ask for in this negotiation who is *a bit* more confident than you? Or someone with *a bit* more experience? Or someone *a bit* more arrogant? Once you have thought of what that thing is, I can almost certainly guarantee that that is the thing you should be asking for.

Holding your nerve in negotiations

The trouble with all this, of course, is that you must be prepared to walk away. And you need to know the reality of your own situation and your own skills. Are you *really* in a negotiating position? Do you *really* know what this work is worth? Are you *really* worth that fee? As a beginner in stand-up comedy, for example, it's pointless asking for the hundreds of pounds that the headliner might be getting paid when you have six months' experience and you are lucky to get the opening slot and be paid £10. That is not the time to bust out the private-jet move. On the other hand, if you know that you are going to be short-changing yourself, incurring costs in your working life and driving yourself mad as you struggle with being undervalued, then in many working situations you must ask for more or walk away. (I can assure you that I have not read *The Art of the Deal* by Donald Trump and I never intend to read *The Art of the Deal* by Donald Trump. Any similarities to his negotiation methods and what I'm prescribing here are purely coincidental. And indicative of the fact that we are both a bit bastardy and it's something you need to learn to be, too.)

A lot of this is about boundaries: knowing what you want and knowing what you are prepared to accept. Making sure you are not being short-changed – by yourself or by others. In the long term you learn that you don't have to take a piece of work just because it is a piece of work and that if something is not really worth your while, then you are just delaying the inevitable. We cannot remain underpaid and undervalued for any prolonged amount of time. We become stressed, depressed and, at the really sharp end of things, unable to work. In the case of freelancers or entrepreneurs, if you set your financial bar too low, you may create an environment where you are not able to make enough money long term. By avoiding negotiation, you're just delaying failure. If you don't ask for what you're worth now, when are you planning to start? If we are able to set realistic boundaries about what we are and aren't prepared to do, then we head off these difficulties in advance. Know your worth. Cultivate your worth. Ask for better. Hope for more. Try and build situations where you feel appreciated and valued – and if that is not possible where you are, find another place.

This way of thinking is about sometimes being more grown-up than we want to be. It's about avoiding complaining and blaming other people. ('Why are they so rubbish? Why can't they just pay more money? Why are they evil?') And it's about not descending into a boring internal narrative of excuses that will allow you to be treated worse than you deserve. ('I'm not good enough.' 'If I was the right person, they would come to me instead of me having to go to them.' 'If there was more money they would have offered it to me already.' 'Someone will get this who is better connected/has a better CV/ deserves it more.' Et cetera.) We all know what these stupid excuses are. In any case, there are so many reasons why you may not get a job or why things may not go your way. So just ask the hell for what you want. And know in your heart that you are prepared to walk away and get something better somewhere else. There is always another option.

CLIMB

● There is endless research proving that in most situations women accept whatever money they are offered and men negotiate. I'm sure there are exceptions to this, and hats off to you if you're one of the women who ask for more. But we all need to work on this: when a sum of money is offered it is called an 'offer' because it is an 'offer'. You do not have to accept an 'offer'. You can see what else might be possible. The other person can always say no to your request and you can always revert to the original offer.

● The reason we don't challenge 'offers' is because we are afraid that the other person will think we are greedy, foolish, unrealistic, grabby or just plain mad. And also perhaps because we don't want to put them in the awkward position of having to say no. This is all about the avoidance of discomfort, some of which exists entirely in our imaginations. Embrace discomfort. Remember that many of our fears are imaginary. (The person is unlikely to think you are greedy. They will probably think, 'Good for her, asking for more, I would too.')

● Rejection is not personal. Rejection is just a no. And often no means 'Not now,' or 'Maybe later,' or 'We'll see,' or 'I don't have all the information.' Rejection is part of life. The entrepreneur Tim Ferriss advises getting used to rejection by asking for a discount every time you buy something in a shop. Every time. Clearly you are not going to get the discount. (Although, he says, you'd be surprised.) But you get used to rejection and to handling the feelings of awkwardness when the other person looks at you as if you are mad. I really recommend this. It is a fascinating psychological exercise to see how different people respond to it. Often they love the brazen nature of it and give you stuff. (Hello, perfume counter.)

LIFT

● Share information and knowledge with other women about money and negotiation. Of course, this is a sensitive subject, especially in certain industries. So you may need to do this with discretion and be careful who you trust. But we all need to open up a little bit more about these things so that we know what to expect and where the money is.

● Of course, if you are in a leadership position – or in a position where you can affect someone's salary – you cannot just randomly go around giving everyone loads of money. (Although, if you do decide to do this, please bear me in mind.) But you can affect the culture of the company, ask other people in senior, decision-making positions the right questions, be nosy about systems and be aggressive about a sense of fairness.

● Do as you would be done by in all things. If you are responsible for anyone being paid, think, 'How would I want to be treated fairly in this situation? What would represent a bonus or a reward to make me feel valued?' It's not always possible to grant these things, but at least if we think about what being treated well looks like, we are halfway there. Once you put a number on something – whether it's for yourself or for someone else – it's easier to work towards it.

5

How to Conquer 'Hepeating'
and Being Interrupted
in Meetings

'It's about getting in the room, getting in the meetings, getting on the list . . . and it doesn't get any easier . . . [even] as you feel that you should be climbing up the ladder.'

Sam Taylor-Johnson

The fight to take status in meetings is the one biggest problem that emerges when I talk to women privately and in events about communication as they attempt to climb. They feel that they are interrupted, sometimes by other, more confident women, sometimes by men. They also report the controversially (but possibly not unfairly) named 'hepeating' – when a man repeats an idea that a woman has already voiced but no one seemed to hear. (Also known as 'invisible woman' syndrome, 'selective deafness', 'selective attention' or 'the cocktail party effect'.)

Sometimes it can feel like every single person you work with is like David Brent from the TV show *The Office*: they don't listen to you, they are only ever waiting for a gap in the conversation so that they can speak themselves; they suck all the air out of the room. The David Brents of this world have no self-awareness, no idea of how they come across to others and no desire to help you be heard. And they are everywhere. There is a ton of very serious academic research on this but none that really proves anything conclusive about gender. Most of the research is into human hearing: it is proven, for example, that babies are able to recognize a parent's voice amongst other voices. We also tend to pick out names (especially, surprise, surprise, our own) and taboo words. So one way to get the attention of someone who's not listening is to preface everything you say with their name and throw in some taboo words: 'Steve, listen the fuck up to this.' See how that goes down. I'm only partly joking.

There are tips and tricks to deal with being interrupted. There are two methods you can experiment with, depending on how bold you're feeling. The first is the simplest. Use the device of 'Thank you'. This is where you divert the attention in a meeting back on to yourself by opening with the words 'thank you' and reclaim the direction of the conversation or the idea. So you say: 'Thank you for expressing it like that. That's exactly what I meant earlier when I was saying . . .' 'Thank you – you totally get it. That is an extension of the point I was raising before . . .' 'Thank you for putting it that way. It's like you read my mind. Here's what I was thinking . . .' (OK, that one is going a bit too far. But you get the picture.)

The second way to pull focus on to you, particularly if you can feel yourself getting emotional and unsure of your voice, is to make sure that whatever you are about to say to interrupt the interrupter starts with a consonant, and the harder the consonant the better: 'Great idea . . .' 'What springs to mind for me . . .' 'Let me summarize what you're saying . . .' 'That's a great point . . .' And hit that word hard as it comes out of your mouth, in the way a teacher might hit a word hard if they were trying to get the attention of a class. When you know that you are feeling weak and annoyed and that emotion might be seeping into your voice, an interruption that starts with a vowel can underline the hesitancy you're feeling: 'I . . . just wanted to say . . .' 'Excuse me . . .' 'Everything you say . . .' Say the consonant examples and the vowel examples out loud and you will hear the difference. This doesn't mean to say that you can never use a word beginning with a vowel when you start speaking in public (that would be weird). The consonant trick is just an easy way to remember to push your voice forward and be definite in what you're saying. Plosive consonants in particular (p, t, k, b, d, g) are very good for producing this effect.

But there is a much easier solution to not getting heard in meetings: we must advocate for each other. Listen up for when others are not being heard and help them out. This is an essential fix, as I'm not sure anyone can take on the David Brents of this world on their own

(Ricky Gervais's creation in *The Office* being the archetypal serial interrupter who always talks over others). The trouble with trying to stand up to people in the David Brent mould is that you can come across as passive aggressive. It's hard to keep control of your emotions in direct confrontation. So enlist help by getting someone else to call out the thing you're having a problem with. It's a genius solution. (Not mine. But I now bring it up all the time.) Obviously, this fix can only work in situations where there are more than two people in a meeting. You get one of the other people to pick up on what is going on and call it out. Or you appoint yourself as the person who will not tolerate others being interrupted or ignored. This is the professional equivalent of another moment of great fear and tension in our lives: the one when you are a teenager and you get someone to go up to someone you like at the school disco and say, 'My friend fancies you.' In the work equivalent you do not get someone to say in a meeting, 'My friend has a problem with all of you. Let me tell you exactly what that problem is.' (Although I would really like it if people started to do this.) The advocate option is where you use them to back you up on the things you've been noticing. Or you decide to become the advocate yourself. There's no need to tell anyone you're going to do this or to wear a T-shirt that says: 'I will make sure no one talks over you today'. It needs to be done discreetly.

How does this work practically? Ahead of the meeting, say to your advocate: 'I might be imagining this, but I think Steve keeps interrupting me and I can't get myself heard. Can you intervene if you see this happening?' And in the meeting the other person might say: 'Steve, what you're saying is really interesting. But can we come back to it? I don't think Jane has finished.' (You are Jane, by the way. I've always wanted to be called Jane.) Alternatively, the other person might help you see if you are being oversensitive or paranoid: 'I saw that happening, but Steve interrupts everyone and doesn't listen to anyone. It's not just you. Maybe someone needs to have a word with his manager.' (Steve could equally be a woman, by the way. No offence to anyone called Steve. I have never wanted to be called Steve.)

The issue with Steve is something you could mention to a colleague, to someone senior to you or to the person chairing the meeting. Get it out in the open, discreetly, outside of the room. This is a way of warning other people that you could do with an advocate. Also, you could ask if you could chair the meeting instead, just to see how you perform in a different role and in order to observe things from the outside. Generally, observing things at work from the outside is very helpful: many of the things that we interpret as personal slights are other people 'acting out' and they're not aimed at us personally. When we interpret them personally we start 'acting out' ourselves because we've taken offence. Then the whole thing goes into a vicious, personal cycle as we recoil or lash out at them. The key is to break the cycle and start behaving more like grown adults with independent ideas and ambitions and less like siblings who are all competing for the attention of our parents. (Which is, of course, what we are all doing most of our lives – making up for stuff that didn't work out in our childhoods or repeating patterns from those times.)

Advocating for others and creating a climate of mutual responsibility takes the heat out of difficult meeting moments. It's the opposite of what we see in television depictions of office life or politics, although you might see it on *The West Wing* or its Danish equivalent, *Borgen* (featuring a female prime minister), two TV shows which show women being listened to in meetings. (Both are worth studying for the body language and communication methods of their female characters.) People getting their point across and not being interrupted is not something we often see in a television show because it's not very dramatic and TV loves drama and conflict. That fact is interesting in itself and it's useful to have in mind when you're experiencing a degree of tension: 'What can I do to de-escalate the drama and conflict? What would make a scene so inoffensive that no one would ever use it in a TV drama? How can I make this *boring*?' No one actively wants to be boring but sometimes it's good to operate on just one level. And if you can find a 'boring' and non-confrontational way of fixing something that is driving you mad . . . well, that's the sweet spot.

The advocate method works particularly well because it's almost impossible to tackle 'hepeating' without sounding like a three-year-old saying, 'But I said that five minutes ago.' (Which is, of course, exactly what you would say, if you could.) It's easy for another person in a meeting to say, 'That's interesting. Let's hear Jane on that.' (Notice a lot of these 'advocate' interventions start with the words, 'That's interesting.' Which is not-so-secret code for 'IDIOT ALERT'.) Or your advocate can add: 'Jane mentioned a similar thing earlier. Jane, what were you saying about that?' (I'm really bigging up Jane here, but I think we can all agree that she deserves it.) This idea of advocacy is one of the most important aspects of lifting as you climb. Not only does it mean that everyone gets heard, everyone feels supported, everyone knows that someone has got their back, it also means that a standard has been established in working culture: 'We listen.' 'We call it out when people are interrupted.' 'We give people credit for their ideas.' That is a culture in which everyone can thrive. And it's easy behaviour to copy. It's so simple: just appoint yourself as The Person for Making Sure Rarely Heard Colleagues Are Not Interrupted, safe in the knowledge that there will be someone else around the table who will do the same for you when the time comes. Do not charge me for the gigantic business card you will need for your new unofficial job title, please.

Why can't we all just be nice?

The word 'nice' has acquired a very bad reputation when it comes to women and work. This is sad, as the last thing the world needs at the moment is for fewer people to be nice. What's so wrong with being nice? Nice is sweetness and kindness. It's the defusing of anger. It's a way to puncture heat and hostility. But we are not supposed to be nice any more, especially as women, as it is seen as a sign of weakness. Some of this thinking is fair comment. We have all realized that a lot of women are unconsciously focused on people-pleasing, being pleasant and making sure they don't do resting bitch face (the neutral expression on a woman's face in repose). It's tempting to get very annoyed about all this and think, 'Don't assume I'm a people-pleaser just because I'm a woman' (I don't know about you, but it's my unwitting default) or 'Why should I smile all the time? I will do resting bitch face if I want.' Where we sit with societal niceness at the moment is awkward. No woman wants to be caught in a trap of unconscious behaviour that perpetuates the status quo. But at the same time we have all grown up in this culture and we all mimic the norms of this culture, or at least most of us do, and one of the norms of our culture is that women are generally nice and can be relied upon to oil the wheels of social interaction. It can be hard to be the person who breaks through this expectation without coming across as hostile. The opposite of niceness is assertive behaviour and that, in women, is often – wrongly – read as 'aggressive'. How do we stop that happening? Should we even care? And why get rid of 'niceness'? Some of these societal norms have evolved for a reason. These expectations are part of the fabric of our lives. And sometimes they're useful. Not only can 'niceness' be advantageous, it also makes life more pleasant. On the flipside, though, there are the haunting words of one of the employees who came forward in the Harvey Weinstein case: 'I learned the social benefits of being deferential, polite and well behaved.' These behaviours are fine if they serve us. They are not fine if they work against us. Investigating where we sit with 'niceness' in different situations is one way of lifting ourselves. It sets a boundary: 'I'm pre-pared to be "nice" up to a point . . .' It's also a way of lifting others: it shows other women that it's OK to be straightforward, assertive, clear. We need to see more women embodying these qualities to understand that they are not the same as being 'mean' or 'a bitch'. They can be neutral behaviours.

Sometimes you can find yourself having to defend 'niceness' and 'likeability' as they have acquired such a bad reputation. In the abstract, we need more niceness – and kindness and sensitivity – not less, as we seem increasingly to live in a culture where people are prepared to be very rude to each other, especially online. But in most specific contexts, women are less able to climb by being excessively pleasant and by always putting the feelings of others above their own. This is the curse that the writer Suzanne Moore describes as 'the dreadful need to be liked'. Of course, no one wants to be disliked. And no one should take pleasure in being disliked. But often we must be prepared to be disliked if we are going to lead, or ask for more, or do a good job, or if we want change of any kind. This is the only way to climb: know in your own mind what is 'nice enough' and what feels like doormat behaviour. By striking this balance, we lift others by example. It is possible to achieve things without being cold-hearted or mean. It is possible to lead with kindness but without being a pushover. This does require intense self-knowledge and self-awareness. Sometimes your version of 'kind enough' may not look kind to others. Sometimes you might be criticized for not being tough enough but you know that you have acted as 'tough' as you want. Learning to trust your own evaluation of your behaviour, without needing the approval of others, is an invaluable life skill to acquire – and one to model for others to copy, even if they might be disapproving of your behaviour. We can be kind-hearted and generous to each other whilst recognizing that these words mean different things to different people. And we do not have to approve of the behaviour of others in order to admire them or be inspired by them. For example, I don't entirely approve of the self-denial and life choices adopted by Olympic skiers. But I admire their tenacity and am inspired by their achievements.

When it comes to being afraid that you will be judged to be 'not nice', I tend to brazen it out. I am happy for people to think I am aggressive. It's OK for them to think that because I know that I'm not, and I'm OK with the level of assertiveness I'm displaying. That other people might potentially think I am aggressive is the price that I pay for being in the room. (I should not have to pay any price for being in the room, but that is just how things are.) You may not be interested in being deliberately 'not nice' but instead be well disposed towards people who take the trouble to be nice, kind and soft in a world that is full of things that are really horrible, cruel and hard. But you cannot let a fondness for niceness play you for a fool. The more you know your own definition of what 'plenty nice enough' feels like for you, the more comfortable this becomes.

It's not easy to find a way through this either/or thinking where you appear to have a choice between being a bitch and being a pushover, and you don't want to occupy either of those roles. It has become a truism for feminists in recent decades to embrace ambition and to stop being coy about what they want. You'll find chapter and verse on this kind of thinking in Lois P. Frankel's *Nice Girls Don't Get the Corner Office: 101 Unconscious Mistakes Women Make That Sabotage Their Careers*. We have come full circle on this stuff: women are supposed to think simultaneously that they shouldn't have to apologize for anything (because why should you have to keep checking your behaviour – men don't have to) and that there's nothing wrong with apologizing anyway. No sooner did everyone absorb all the messages from Sheryl Sandberg about 'leaning in' (from the book *Lean In: Women, Work and the Will to Lead* by the Chief Operating Officer of Facebook) than they were complaining that organizations shouldn't make it necessary for women to lean in in the first place ('Why don't they bend to encompass us? Why do we have to do the work of adapting to them?') and that it might make more sense to 'lean out'. And, hey, maybe no one should be taking lessons from Facebook, a company with plenty of very public organizational challenges. It is all incredibly confusing.

Virtually every time I go to an event in an organization where these themes are being discussed, people say they really want to change because things are not working out for them. But they also say: 'I refuse to change. This is the way I am. I'm not putting on an act. I thought authenticity was really important nowadays.'

They want things to be different but they don't want to undertake the action that will create change. This leaves everyone in an impossible bind. The way most people get around this – both men and women – is by blaming everyone that they work with and assuming that if only those people would act differently, then everything would be fine. Very few people are keen to change their own behaviour because they want to 'be themselves'. At the same time, women are reminded that they might be suffering from 'imposter syndrome' – the idea that you're not up to the job and you're about to be revealed as a fraud. Equally, women are told to avoid people-pleasing. And we are encouraged to curb our niceness completely. And yet all three of these behaviours are often the cornerstones of many women's personalities and women get a lot out of these behaviours. Imposter syndrome, while it has many downsides, can be a sign of humility and self-awareness. Who wants to work with someone who never has self-doubt? Similarly, people-pleasing can be self-defeating, but the positive side of it is empathy and altruism. 'Niceness' is not fashionable. But we need nice people everywhere: they are the ones who bring in the biscuits. Don't get rid of the biscuits.

Whenever I talk to women in corporate settings about how these behaviours are affecting their work and how they see themselves, they are often completely paralysed. Are they supposed to stop apologizing completely and 'be like men'? Or should they find a way to 'be authentic' and stop second-guessing themselves? How can they be ambitious and feminine at the same time? These are questions I have heard women ask many times. And it is one of the most important questions of our working lives. What do ambition and power look like when they're not exclusively masculine? What does a mix of powers look like when part of it is the old-fashioned 'power' model and part of it is soft skills like persuasion and kindness? We don't know what this looks like in action as the power model of the last few thousand years has only started to be challenged in the last one hundred years. No wonder we are finding it difficult to work this out. We are still building it. It is a work-in-progress. We must find ways – together – of supporting each other in investigating these 'no right answer' questions for ourselves and of defining what leadership looks like, what kindness looks like, what toughness looks like. Because they look different in everyone. The way to lift as we climb is to encourage ourselves and other women when we see these experiments happening. This change can happen in tiny, invisible ways. Like giving yourself a pat on the back every time you send a non-apologetic, succinct email. Or it can be big and scary. Like speaking up for a colleague who is too afraid to tackle a difficult issue at work on her own. Or it can even be medium-sized. Like responding to a situation in a neutral, balanced and objective way instead of 'being nice' or 'being aggressive'.

How gendered is this, really?

I am wary of people who paint this as a 'men versus women' problem. The patriarchal ways of looking at power, communication and how we relate to each other are shared by all of us and fostered by all of us. They might benefit some members of society more than others but we've all been upholding them for hundreds of years. Also, we all know from anecdotal and personal experience that many, many people operate outside the norm. We all know women who have many supposedly masculine traits, and vice versa. No one really fits into the averages that we pretend are ruling our lives. A lot of this thinking is about picking apart how you sit with social conditioning and working out what you know feels right to you as a person. We all choose our behaviour and our reactions every moment of the day. If someone insults you, you can either take it as that or you can think, 'That person is trying to insult me. But the insult has nothing to do with me, it belongs to them.' Then you can think, 'Do I deserve this insult?' If the answer is no, let it go. It's about the other person and is their problem. That response is not gendered and anyone can do it.

The temptation to diagnose these social behaviours

and cultural norms as an exclusively gendered problem is huge. Whilst there's no denying the structural in-equalities women face, and there's a raft of evidence of gender-based discrimination, I think we have to be care-ful not to set up a war. I would argue that that has been tried and it hasn't worked. The second wave of feminism blamed 'the patriarchy' for most of the problems women faced. And most people understood 'the patriarchy' to mean 'men'. Decades later, the attitude persists in some quarters that 'men need to change'. This position doesn't acknowledge the fact that we all uphold these social norms. We are all a product of the patriarchy. Many men also feel crushed and exhausted by 'alpha culture' and the sharp-elbowed race to the top. This is a problem that must be faced jointly, even if it's initially hard to get others to join in. Also, I haven't come across any research that proves conclusively, for example, that women are less likely to be listened to than men, so we should be cautious of eating up the anecdotal evidence surrounding these kinds of ideas. It's true that there are difficulties in this area, but once you start thinking, 'I'm a woman and so no one listens to me anyway,' then all is lost. We all know what is being talked about when we mention 'hepeating', but we all know colleagues who are women who are also likely to take credit for our ideas, and bosses of both genders who are not able to give the limelight to their underlings. We also all know people who are prone to insulting others and we can see from the outside that their propensity to issue insults has very little to do with the people to whom the insults are directed and everything to do with the person they're coming from. (Not that I am looking at any prominent world leaders at the moment.)

What people ask themselves when they are preparing for meetings and difficult encounters is 'How can I maintain control when someone else has offended me?' This is about the ego under attack. Our instinct is to think, 'The other person should not have attacked me in the first place.' Or not made you feel small, or not made you feel ignored. We make it about them and what they should have done, instead of thinking, 'I can choose to shrug this off.' Or smiling and thinking, 'That person behaves like that with everyone, not just with me.' You want to avoid continually going into situations where you have 'And another thing . . . !' written all over your face. It's hard for other people to empathize with you or support you if you are bringing too much emotion into the situation, let alone the idea that you are looking for vengeance.

I was once at an event with a group of senior executive women where one was talking about her frustration with her bosses. They didn't recognize her talent, they ignored her suggestions for improvement, they had failed to pick up on any of her hints about the fact that she was unhappy in her role and wanted more responsibility. The group discussed her options and got her to think about the different things she could try to move things forward, but the conversation was going in circles. Suddenly I saw the one solution that would fix everything for her: 'You could always torch the place.' She laughed. But it needed saying: the way she was describing her workplace, it was the only logical out-come. Destroy them, burn them, make them pay. It was what she was saying without saying it. I don't blame anyone for thinking this way: many of us suffer years and years of hurt at the hands of employers and col-leagues who just don't seem to care about anything (and certainly don't care about us) and it's hard to know how to swing things your way.

Once my invitation to arson was out in the open (you're welcome), we could move on; we had acknow-ledged the depth and the extremity of her emotion – and the impossibility of staying in that emotion because it would result in disaster, in violence and in death. (As I say, you're welcome.) This is an example of the 'Yes, and . . .' principle from improvisational comedy. This is a way of thinking about a situation which is logical but not necessarily possible in real life. (For example, 'I hate my boss.' 'Yes! And you could murder him!' 'Yes! And I could dance on his grave!' 'Yes! And you could make cocaine dust out of his ashes and snort it!' You see why this is not necessarily possible in real life.) In the torch-ing example, if you accept that the woman's situation is deeply intolerable and that the people around her deserve to be punished, then the next logical step (in a fictional world with no real-world consequences) is to destroy them all. Sometimes our subconscious mind is going to this place when we talk about the people we work with. This is what happens when we are guided by our emotions. They take us to dark places. Then we must try to apply logic because we know that we cannot actually act on those extreme emotions. This is why meetings are often bland and nothing happens. Or they explode. It's also why many people drink heavily after work. Solution? Admit your emotions to yourself. Find a way to get them out before you take them into a meeting. Vent to a more experienced, trusted colleague. Force yourself to write a list of possible outcomes. See how you might compromise or find another way forward before you go into a meeting. It might never come to that, but at least you've already thought through how you will handle it. The trouble with many work situations is that under the surface we are living out impossibly dark emotions. And on the surface we are having to be ridiculously polite.

The key to all of this is taking the emotion out of situations. Most things in life could be fixed if everyone took them less personally. Often when people ask me about dealing with meetings, especially about being interrupted or other people stealing their ideas, I can see the heat in their face even as they talk about it. Just remembering it and articulating it is enough to bring back the negative emotions of that moment. I'm not suggesting we pretend to ourselves that it's fine to be offended or ignored or overlooked and that we should put a brave face on it. We have to admit to ourselves how strongly we feel about these things and allow ourselves time to be offended, to be insulted, to grieve for our inability to fight back and find a solution, to be hurt that no one else came to our assistance. Once you've admitted the feeling, you can choose how to react. Did you really need to feel insulted? Is there another interpretation? It is possible to 'rehearse' taking things more calmly and less personally by taking a step back mentally, both by preparing better for meetings and by dealing with our feelings appropriately afterwards (whether by venting to a colleague or attacking a cushion). But that self-discipline takes practice. If you are full of anger, there's no point in ignoring it. Unless we experience these feelings and give in to them – privately, alone or with a trusted friend – then they fester. And every time you're back in that situation, they will return. If they come up even when you are asked a question about it (and I see this happening all the time) then you haven't dealt with those feelings. And until you've dealt with them, you are not in a calm enough frame of mind to fix the situation.

CLIMB

● The best overall fix for changing your behaviour and the behaviour of others in meetings can sometimes be to do nothing for a while. Get used to being silent and watching and waiting. Especially if you have repeated patterns in your work (a meeting every Monday morning, for example), allow yourself three or four weeks where you sit back and observe what happens, naturally and without judgement. This is a useful habit because (a) you get used to neutral observation, which can often be a handy tool in life and (b) if you are not focused on participating and how you're being treated, you start to notice all sorts of interesting things about the dynamics in play. This kind of observation shows you where the flaws are, and that they may have nothing to do with you. It allows you to start thinking about how others are being treated, too.

● Challenge meeting culture in your place of work. And challenge it in every group dynamic where you feel you are not being heard. If you have a group of friends at work where no one ever listens to you and you get pushed to the back, get a new group of friends. Socialize with a different department. Or organize a social event where you are the one in charge. At work, ask if you can run a meeting, just to shake things up or for the experience or for the practice. Do not wait to be asked. And outside of work, do not wait for your friends to change. They are not going to change.

● Watch people you work with whose behaviour you admire and try to absorb bits of it. Who behaves well in meetings? Be like them. Who speaks well? Be like them. Ask them how they prepare and how they get over feelings of self-consciousness.

● Ask if you can be in the room even as an observer. Many women report that there are meetings and rooms they can't get into. There is a good (unspoken, unconscious) reason why you are not in that room, so it is not going to be an easy deadlock to break. Being straightforward can work: 'I know I'm not excluded from this meeting, so I'd like to sit in.' Your next step is to manage the transition from onlooker to participant. Some people feel wary about being in meetings where they say nothing and don't contribute. But you can't make a difference to a set-up until you understand how it works. You don't expect to act in a play before you have seen many other plays, learned your lines and rehearsed. (Not to mention that in a play you have a director and a supporting cast.) Why would you expect to go into a meeting for the first time and blow everyone away?

LIFT

● Advocate, advocate, advocate. This is the right thing to do and it's also useful in so many situations. If you are feeling tired or you don't have much to say on a particular day, use this meeting to highlight the contribution of others. You can spend an entire meeting just doing traffic control. Who has spoken? Who hasn't been heard? Who was cut off? You don't have to be the chair to do this.

● If you have authority or status, lend it to others. Let someone else sit in your position as chair occasionally. Delegate. Cede authority. Mix things up. You don't want to undermine your position, but sharing power on occasion makes you look more powerful. Relaxed power is real power. Enforced power is not.

● Talk to people in other organizations about how their meetings work and how they overcome dysfunction and paralysis. For example: I notice a lot of people complaining now about how 'useless' video-conferencing is. They say that no one in the meetings feels heard, that these meetings are difficult to chair, that people only half-listen. I don't know anyone who says: 'Our video-conferencing meetings are working really well.' And yet the use of this technology is spreading. Someone needs to find the person who sings its praises and get them to teach everyone else how to do it efficiently. Otherwise, these meetings need to stop. They are driving decent people crazy.

● Embrace the idea of experimenting to see if it benefits others – if it helps them to be heard, saves their time, smooths interactions. Experiment with challenges and boundaries. Everyone in a meeting has to speak for sixty seconds, and there's a timer. Or everyone has to ask their question or make their point in three sentences. Or everyone has to be silent for thirty seconds (time it) before they speak again. There are so many ways to shake things up, even as a temporary experiment. The meeting is held standing up and will only last five minutes, for example. Mobile phones are banned. Laptops are banned. Taking notes is banned. Or you could spend less time in the meeting discussing things and more time listing what the five action points are. You get the message here. If what you are doing is not working, try something different.

● Did I mention 'advocate'? Listen out for other people being spoken over and ease their path. Watch out for people taking credit for other people's ideas and intervene. If you're a senior person in the room, do something if you see junior people always being asked to make the coffee or take notes. If you're a junior person, hang back a bit before volunteering to do menial things and encourage a climate in which people question whether these things are required at all.

6

How to Get Mentoring Right

'We cannot all succeed when half of us are held back.'
Malala Yousafzai

Many women think that having a mentor is the key to success. And they might be right. Imagine being Oprah Winfrey and having Maya Angelou on speed-dial. That must have been some serious motivation. But in real life there is no point looking for a mentor unless you can answer a couple of really significant questions: Why do you want a mentor? And what are you hoping they'll do for you? It's not fair – or wise – to expect anyone else to be your miracle. Although it is fair – and wise – to ask other people for help. Because often they get a lot out of giving that help and they're glad to be asked. It's a two-way street. I imagine Maya was as happy to hear from Oprah as Oprah was happy to be able to call on Maya. But very often if you drill down into the answers to these two questions, it becomes obvious that what a lot of us crave is not really a mentor but a fairy godmother who will do everything so that we don't have to. Someone who will lift us so that we can give our triceps a rest and stop climbing. Maybe someone who will push all the buttons in the elevator for us and send us straight to the top floor of life.

So there's a conundrum here. We all need and deserve mentors in our working lives. But we have to be realistic about what they can offer us. And they cannot suddenly make everything better. We know this truth and it frustrates us. So instead of navigating it and finding a compromise position, we (or at least I) try to manage everything on our own and be dramatic about how no one is going to help us but ourselves. In reality, it is never true that we are alone in our struggles. It's incredibly tempting to stomp around in an invisible feathered chiffon gown in the imaginary Oscars dressing room in your mind, screaming, 'Well, I suppose if I'm going to get anything done around here, I'm just going to have to do it myself.' But the truth is that help, tips, nuggets of advice and nudges in the right direction are all around us if only we care to see them. There are two extremes at work here. First, the 'magic wand' idea, that having a mentor will solve all your problems. And second, the 'diva' idea, that it's your way or the highway and what does anyone else know anyway? Neither is helpful.

I was a bit trapped in this mentality when I first started performing stand-up comedy. I knew on the one hand that no one could do the work I needed to do on my behalf and that the only way to progress was by learning and 'failing upwards'. On the other hand, I desperately wanted someone else to make it easier for me and I wanted to avoid making the most obvious mistakes. Which is why I asked a very experienced comedian to critique my set after a night when it had gone badly wrong. He thought about it for a long time and then he looked at me and said slowly and thoughtfully, 'Just be funny.' This is not the advice I'd wanted. What he was essentially saying was: 'Don't ask me. Go away and do the work.' Annoyingly, he was right and this was the piece of mentoring I needed at the time. But this is not what any of us is hoping for in a mentor: we are looking for someone who is a cross between our ideal parent and Robin Williams in *Dead Poets Society*. We are not looking for someone who tells us the truth – that we have to fix this for ourselves.

The trick to approaching mentoring in a healthy and realistic way is to be neutral and relaxed about it. We love to feed ourselves the myth about our working lives that everything is extremely complicated and difficult and only someone with an extremely large brain or a great deal of experience, compassion and empathy could possibly know what we're going through. Fortunately, this is not true. Almost everything we experience has been experienced by someone else before us. And nothing is so terrible or so complex that it can't be managed. Plus, the reality is this: we are not as alone as we think we are. Our problems often have an almost obscenely simple solution. A good mentor can really help here. And what that person has to give us does not have to be arcane or mysterious. They might just have the right word at the right time.

Be wary, though, of the fad that mentoring represents. I am a cautious fan of the American entrepreneurial guru Gary Vaynerchuk, who is vehemently opposed to anyone having a mentor. I say 'cautious' because his pronouncements can come across as too much even to his supporters and he is best consumed in small doses lest you start shouting, 'LET'S KEEP THIS SHIT REAL, PEOPLE' into the screen every time you see a smartphone. (Most of his pronouncements consist of him yelling motivational profanities for consumption on social media.) This is something I suspect he knows himself as he releases his words of wisdom to the digital sphere in carefully controlled sixty-second blasts. Vaynerchuk is full of bluster and hyperbole and every other word is an expletive. He's an extreme character but he says some wise things. And his scathing view of mentorship is interesting to think about: 'You don't need a mentor. You need to know yourself.'

His reticence around this topic is correct in my view: he argues that awareness of the self is far more important and valuable than having a mentor. People use 'mentor' as a buzzword, as a signifier for their ambition and how seriously they take themselves. It can have a narcissistic tinge to it. You can imagine someone twirling their hair as they sit back, sipping a cocktail, musing, 'Oh, I wonder who would be a fabulous person to have as my mentor?' And then there's all the drama around it that people love becoming wrapped up in. How will you ask them to be your mentor? What if they say no? Should you use the word 'mentor' or be more coy about it? It turns into a low-grade version of a marriage proposal.

I've been on the receiving end of this kind of 'mentor' request. I've advised others on how to handle relationships with people they regard unofficially or officially as mentors. And I've treated several women and men in my life as mentors, often without them knowing but sometimes semi-officially, signalled by me saying: 'You realize at this point that I am treating you like a mentor? No pressure.' Increasingly, companies have mentorship programmes where they pair senior and junior executives. No matter whether a mentorship is offered to you or whether you seek one out yourself, I'm wary that this can seem like a cringeworthy arrangement. The relationship between a mentor and mentee is a strange power-balance. In the worst circumstances the mentee can feel like a fan or an admirer paying court to the mentor. And I'm extremely wary of the connotations that mentorship has, thanks to a relationship craze I remember from my schooldays, where there was a fad for so-called 'Older Friends' and

'Younger Friends' amongst the girls. (The homoerotic echoes of these labels are clear but, on the surface, there was nothing sexual in it. It really wasn't that exciting.) Girls who were around twelve or thirteen years old would want to have an 'Older Friend' aged fifteen or sixteen. They would write notes to each other and swap gossip. There was a huge amount of kudos in this relationship: if you were attractive and 'cool', then someone would want you as their Younger Friend. I never had an Older Friend and this made me very uncool. It's really important that a mentor is not just someone you gaze up at in admiration. They need to be a real source of candour, support and advice.

The last thing I want to do now, thirty years later, is to be someone's Older Friend. So I have been slightly horrified by requests to become someone's mentor. Conversely, I am never horrified by requests for specific advice. That seems reasonable and I will usually try to respond if I have time. But the few requests I have received for mentoring have come from people who seem to have very little idea about anything that I've done. They will have picked on one thing that I do that they'd like to do (have a certain number of Instagram followers, have a podcast, be on the radio) and they have clearly decided that if they ask me to be their mentor, this achievement will somehow be conferred on to them. It doesn't work like that. In my experience, this is why some women become uncomfortable around the idea of being a mentor: they're worried about what's expected of them and how realistic that expectation is.

In the worst of cases, the mentor quest becomes a vanity project which a mentee embarks upon under the guise of furthering their career or entrepreneurial aims. Instead, it becomes another kind of busywork which uses up valuable time when you could be job-searching, sending out ideas or doing whatever you are supposed to be doing as part of your actual work. Vaynerchuk warns that becoming obsessed with the idea of having a mentor has become a strange contemporary disease. It's a dangerous idea, he says, because having a mentor can replace the one thing that will move you forward: taking risks and gathering information through action. Investing time and energy in seeking mentors, reading all the right self-help books, attending all the right workshops and talking to all the right people can become another form of 'good girl' activity. All to avoid actually doing anything that might teach you some-thing or – horrors! – expose you to failure. I suspect most of us want a mentor so that we can avoid making any mistakes, or so that we can find a shortcut. Get a mentor so that they can make all the mistakes for you, right? Wrong. Avoiding mistakes is a bad idea. And there are no shortcuts to anything worth doing.

That said, it's wrong to demonize the idea of support-ers, cheerleaders or village elders who can champion you on your way – which is exactly what the role of a mentor is. To counteract this cynical view of mentoring? Simply be wary of being complacent. ('I have a mentor! All my problems are solved! I'll never need to go to a job interview again!') Having a mentor is not a silver bullet. It won't suddenly make you motivated or reveal all the secrets of your industry or unlock the best side of you. Nor will it give you an ally in high places who can whisper in the ear of people whose favour you seek. But it should be able to give you a tiny flavour or inkling of these things. The best application of a mentor is as a person to avail you of all your misunderstandings and laugh at your incredibly stupid assumption that you know how things work before you've tried to do them.

One of the most tedious things about any line of work is that you have to be in it to know how things work. And this is one of the places where a mentor or a more experienced colleague can actually shortcut things. When I was younger, for example, I desperately wanted to work 'in fashion'. It took a stint on a magazine for me to realize that working 'in fashion' if you weren't well connected (which I was not) meant working in a cupboard for several months, if not several years. And I mean this literally: when I entered the world of work, editors and assistants literally worked out of 'the fashion cupboard', which was a tiny room where all the clothes that were going to be used on fashion shoots were stored. The main part of the job was calling in these clothes, logging them, schlepping them out to fashion shoots, counting them all back in again on a clipboard and then sending them back to where they came from. From outside the fashion world or the world of magazines, you wouldn't know that this job was the equivalent of being a postman with personal responsibility for designer clothes worth thousands of pounds. I had imagined that working 'in fashion' meant meeting and interviewing fascinating, artistic people and having sparkling conversations. It did not. It meant wielding a clipboard with a list on it of twenty-seven different types of diamante hair slide. If I had had an appropriate mentor, I might have learned this and realized that I was not committed enough to be in that world and stick at the grunt work. I didn't want it badly enough. A mentor would have disabused me of the notion that this was the path for me in the space of a couple of questions.

Similarly, as a young woman, I thought that being a foreign correspondent for newspapers or television meant you had to speak the foreign language of the country where you were posted and have an in-depth knowledge of that particular place. It doesn't. It means the opposite: it means you can be parachuted into any territory and report on the news story of the moment. It also means you only report from that country with the sensibility of the country you are reporting for. As a veteran foreign correspondent eventually told me, if you are in Amsterdam, you are less interested in stories about politics or crime or culture and far more interested in whether there is a tulip shortage or a slowdown in clog production or a run on hash brownies. If I had had a proper mentor in the early years, I probably could have condensed the first ten years of my career into a few days. A mentor is a hotline to behind-the-scenes information. And they can help you to see two things that are indecently helpful. First, your next immediate move, or how to choose between several options presenting themselves. And, second, the bigger picture.

Your mentor needs to be the right person and the mentoring needs to be for the right reasons. I once had a meeting with a woman who was determined to have me as her mentor. In some ways, I was flattered because it's a compliment if someone looks up to you and thinks that you can help them. However, it quickly became clear that she wasn't really sure why she was asking me. The most obvious question for me was this: 'Why do you want me to be your mentor?' I didn't feel that she had an answer to this other than, 'You seem successful' – this is a dangerous assumption in itself as we never know the truth of someone else's life – 'and I want to be successful too.' 'You've got stuff that I want' is not a good enough reason to have someone as your mentor. It's also a real sign that you're not asking the right questions. This person should have been asking me, for example, about whether the aspects of my life and work that looked successful from the outside really were successful. A proper mentor is the sort of person you can share that stuff with.

There are many aspects of other people's lives that are not as they seem. From the outside, you will not know their salary, their living arrangements, their contacts, their upbringing, how much they spend on childcare, how much time they spend on social media, what outside help they hire, and so on. I have had many experiences of people contacting me to ask about how you get published as a writer of books or newspaper articles, how you have a 'successful' podcast (whatever this means) or how you have a 'successful' Edinburgh show (whatever this means). In theory, I've done all these things and yet if I am going to have an open conversation with someone about the pros and cons of throwing yourself into these competitive worlds, then I need to know that they have some kind of basic understanding of what it is going to cost them in terms of money, energy and emotions. Otherwise it's not a serious conversation and it's not a serious mentorship. There are many times that I have talked to people, for instance, about the decisions that you have to make when putting on an Edinburgh show and I can see their eyes glazing over when they realize how much work and risk is involved. Similarly, because I have three children I have had a lot of conversations over the years about how I 'juggle' (shudder) work and children. People do not want to hear that I have never had a day's maternity leave, that I can often work through weekends and holidays or that I can also go a whole week without being able to do any work because one of my children is sick. And they don't want to hear about the childcare that I have used (and had to find ways of paying for) over the past fifteen years. For me, that is the kind of thing that is useful to know from 'mentors': how to earn money flexibly, how to negotiate better rates, how to find creative solutions and stay upbeat when all your childcare falls through or one of your clients goes bankrupt.

Similarly, I am constantly surprised at the number of people who say they are interested in things that they don't really want to do. People who will attend an event about writing a book but will never actually write a book. People who will go on about doing a podcast for years but never actually make a podcast. Curiosity is great, but why waste your curiosity on something that you don't feel that committed to? Spend the time investigating something you might actually do.

How to get the most out of mentoring

The most productive way to handle mentoring is to manage your expectations and be clear what the relationship is. One of the best ways I've found to tick the 'lift as you climb and don't end up in hell' box is to mentor people unofficially. I try to behave towards women who are starting out as if I am their mentor; they just don't know it yet. This is never a bad thing to do, but don't expect any thanks, and beware of giving people unsolicited advice. This has been more productive and satisfying in my experience than taking on some semi-official role. I've had a few pointless experiments with teenagers doing 'work experience' with me where I've taken them to amazing meetings and they have just stared at the floor, bored, haven't asked a single question or attempted to form a connection with a person who would be in a position to give them a job. (Something I find extraordinary, as when I was younger I would have literally killed someone to get a meeting with anyone who could give me a job in journalism.)

Inside a mentoring relationship – especially one that has been set up for you by your company, as is increasingly happening – one of the most useful things you can do is to look out for unexpected information, especially things that you don't want to hear. One of the best pieces of advice I've ever had is from TED talker and former tech CEO Margaret Heffernan. I regard her as a personal mentor, although I don't think she knows this as I have never actually told her. She has not worked in the same kind of jobs as I have. She has hired and fired hundreds of people and I am a lone ranger. We do have, however, a similar mindset. That is what makes her a good mentor: she always understands that the mechanics of the work situations that I face are far less important than how I feel about them. She once told me something I have never forgotten: that the one thing I need to do in my career is to make sure that I keep having fun: 'Above all, look for fun. Without it, everything gets pointless very quickly.'

When she told me this I was thinking, 'What kind of mentoring is that? "Look for fun"? It's my career. It's not a children's television programme.' It seemed too simple. But the more I thought about it, the more I realized that she was right. If something is no fun to you, it is not going to sustain your interest for very long. Fun is also great as a deciding factor because it's so subjective: only you can know what your definition of fun is. The idea felt self-indulgent to me for a long time. ('Work is not supposed to be fun. That's why it's work.') But as I've got older I've used it increasingly as a way of deciding between things ('Which of these is more fun for me?') and as a way of knowing what I can more easily say no to. Of course, not everything can be fun. Because we all have responsibilities and we all have to do things we don't want to do. But ultimately, this is genius advice. You cannot continue indefinitely on a career path that is no fun for you.

If mentoring can teach you something surprising and unexpected that you might not have been able to find out for yourself, then that is the best kind of short cut. It's vital to look at mentoring in a clear-eyed way, though. Just as no job is the magic answer to all your problems (and no boss is either), a mentor is not your fairy godmother or the Wizard of Oz. (And remember what the Wizard of Oz turned out to be: an empty promise.) A good mentor helps you see the way through when things are difficult but reminds you that it is not supposed to be easy. A really good mentor will tell you that all this may not be in your control anyway. We do know that our actions have consequences and that we are capable of helping ourselves whilst helping others at the same time. However, recent research suggests that very little may be within our control – and that even the things that go well for us are more a matter of luck than design. This sounds depressing – we want to believe that we have some control, otherwise what's the point in trying to achieve anything? But if it's true, then it's something we need to know about.

In his book *Success and Luck: Good Fortune and the Myth of Meritocracy*, the economist Robert H. Frank makes the argument that successful and wealthy people are biased towards the belief that they deserve their success and wealth because they worked hard and/or they are extremely talented. He points out that the latest social science research indicates that chance plays a far bigger role in determining important life outcomes than human beings like to acknowledge. He calls this the 'myth of meritocracy'. This myth has become exceptionally powerful in the self-help industry: if you take matters into your own hands, take consistent action, then you can't help but achieve results. We all want this to be true because we all want to be able to shape our futures, just as we all want a cheerleader on our side who is going to send things soaring in the direction we want.

It can't do any harm to take consistent action to affect your prospects. And it can't do any harm to consult with a sensible, intelligent mentor. It makes sense that these steps might help you. But it's also true that you will need luck to be on your side. If you are born with the capacity to concentrate and apply yourself (or you are able to learn how to do that), then that's good fortune. If you have the resources which allow you to thrive, that's also good fortune. And if you stumble upon the right mentor at the right moment, it's more by luck than design.

CLIMB

● Set a timer for five minutes and make a list of all the people who have been unofficial mentors to you in your life and work. Teachers, coaches, relatives, friends, colleagues. The purpose of this exercise is to help you see all the 'angels' out there. (Not to get too woo-woo about this.) There are many unofficial mentors in our lives. We rarely admit this to ourselves or acknowledge it.

● Be open to the idea of unofficial mentors. Is there anyone whose expertise you could mine more fully? Do they need to know you're doing that or can you do it informally?

● If you feel you want an official arrangement with someone, find a way to make this happen. Who can you approach for an open conversation where you say the words, 'Would you consider mentoring me? We can work out a schedule where we meet every three months for half an hour.' Set clear boundaries and expectations so that the other person knows what you are asking of them. (If you are thinking, 'What use is it to me to meet someone for half an hour every three months?' then you might need to rethink your own boundaries and expectations. People are busy! They are not here to serve you!)

● Be careful who you choose as a mentor. You need someone you already know, even if it's as a passing acquaintance. It can look odd to approach someone you don't know: it feels too much like you are using them for their position rather than because of the connection between you.

● If you're lucky enough to be assigned a mentor at work, talk to as many people as possible off the record who have managed this relationship successfully (and unsuccessfully) in the past. Don't expect your mentor to make this arrangement work. Try to set clear expectations and a timetable (how often you meet, the purpose of mentorship). Be open to the relationship surprising you.

LIFT

● Take your list of 'unofficial mentors' and send one, some, or all of them a note letting them know that you've just realized the effect they had on you. Or if you are the sort of person who likes writing testimonials on LinkedIn, then write one of those for them. Do not put yourself into the trap of thinking that it has to be a Shakespearean sonnet. Write three sentences. Send. If you're already thinking, 'Three sentences is not good enough . . .', then resign yourself to the fact that you will not be sending these notes. (Always be careful of 'not good enough'. Done is better than perfect.)

● Offer to be a mentor at your place of work. There are lots of options here. Talk to someone senior at work about how mentoring operates in your organization and volunteer to be a part of it. If it doesn't exist, set it up.

● Mentor outside your work or outside your industry using an existing structure. Google is your friend. (The search term 'offer to be a mentor UK' yields 51 million results.) Maybe you can mentor someone locally who needs interview skills. Or you can mentor someone in your industry who is new and needs support. Many professional bodies offer mentoring schemes.

● Mentor unofficially. Be aware of the fact that some people can feel put off by the term 'mentor' and the expectations it might imply. Look out for colleagues, friends and contacts who might be open to treating you as an unofficial mentor, and be generous with your advice and your time – if this fits in with what's going on in your life. (Do not fall into the trap of being generous when you don't really have the time or bandwidth. There is a season for everything. We all deserve mentors – official and unofficial – who don't begrudge their time.)

● Put out an offer on social media for an intern (paid) or a mentee (unpaid).

7

How to Own Up to Your Mistakes and Help Others to Own Up to Theirs

> *'Women are like tea bags. You never know how strong
> they are until they're in hot water.'*
>
> Eleanor Roosevelt

There is a wonderful moment in the film *Sisters* with Tina Fey and Amy Poehler where they have to collectively tell their parents that they have wrecked their family home. They get through it by owning up together and – miraculously – by not blaming each other. They are only really able to do this because of the hell that they have been through the night before. The swimming pool has become a sinkhole, a tree has fallen on the house, there is blue paint everywhere and a friend of theirs has left the party with the ballerina from a music box stuck up his bottom. When things cannot get any worse and we cannot hide our failure, we are good people. We stop blaming others and looking for excuses and we hold our hands up and say, 'Yes, this happened. It's terrible and I'm sorry. What next?'

It shouldn't take a man getting a plastic ballet dancer stuck up his rear end for us to get to this point. But in real life we all know that people don't like taking responsibility for their mistakes. The fear of failure, making a mistake and getting something wrong haunts many women and constantly emerges in feedback and consultations. In public speaking, for example, one of our greatest fears (second only to doing the speaking itself) is the moment where you have to face questions at a Q & A after a presentation and you realize that you genuinely don't know the answer to something. Everyone wants to know how to bluff their way through it and how to support others when you can see them facing a similar situation. Most of all, though, people want to know how to not get anything wrong in the first place. Which is, of course, completely unrealistic. We never know everything. We ought to be comfortable saying, 'I don't know. I'll find out later and get back to you,' or 'I don't know, but I do have the information in my office,' or 'I don't know. Maybe someone else here does.' Or even 'Let's Google that in the break.' But, as I've mentioned before, most people are very scared of admitting ignorance of any kind.

Apportioning blame, accepting responsibility and taking credit are three things - all interlinked - that come up regularly in events and workshops around the topic of public speaking and performance. I've witnessed this many times. Often this is the first question in a session ('How do I say, "I don't know" without looking stupid?'), followed by a cascade of similar questions.

The usual questions around other people sabotaging us – 'What do I do if someone interrupts me in a meeting?' 'How do I stop someone else taking credit for my ideas in meetings?' (questions addressed in Chapter 5) – are accompanied by an equal or bigger fear: the fear of sabotaging ourselves with ignorance or stupidity. This is all about the fear of failure. 'What if I don't know the answer to an important question in a meeting?' 'How do I style out a mistake?' 'What if I screw up really badly?' These things seem to have nothing to do with public speaking, which is usually the given reason why we have gathered. And yet they are always the questions that are close to the surface. What links them is our attitude towards leadership and being assertive and self-assured. If you feel like a competent leader and you are genuinely self-assured, you don't worry about these things. Which led me to realize that the women asking such questions do not feel like leaders and do not feel self-assured. I've seen these questions asked in mixed-gender sessions and in women-only sessions and my evidence is anecdotal, not scientific. But in my experience women talk about these things easily and worry about them a lot. Men are more likely to ask about how to insert humour into a presentation or ask for tips about how to ad lib. If they have fears about making mistakes, they don't often voice them.

These questions around insecurity and 'not knowing' are really about control and what to do if we think we don't have it. Or how to take control in situations that seem difficult. These are the two most challenging moments: one, when things go horribly wrong, and two, when we don't know what the hell we're doing. I've learned about these situations through stand-up comedy. On stage in stand-up there are many situations that you can't control or influence at all and which are not your fault. Equally, there are many elements which you can control and which are your responsibility. For example: is your material good enough, are you well prepared enough, have you set the right expectations for the audience, are you 'giving' enough? But the thing that unites the elements you can control (your preparation, the quality of your act) and the elements you can't (someone in the audience who is very drunk, people in the audience who came to see someone else on the bill) is that whilst they are not all your fault, all these elements are now your responsibility. No one else is going to deal with that drunk person (unless there are bouncers - but you will still probably have to direct them to deal with the person). The people who didn't come for you and may never like your act are not going anywhere. This is the same dilemma as in *Sisters*. No one is going to un-sink the pool, un-crash the car or magic that ballerina away.

These situations are chilling because they are a massive test of the ego. You are being put under a microscope, like an insect undergoing a laboratory experiment. Will you shrink and die? Or will you acti-vate your armour? Will you attack? This sounds dramatic, but this kind of feeling gets played out in work situa-tions on a smaller, less psychologically damaging scale, all the time. You might be in a job interview with three interviewers where you can sense that two of them really like you but the third doesn't. You might be in a work presentation where many of your allies are in the room but the person with the most power is someone who isn't keen on you. You might be in a speaking situ-ation where you are a bit out of your depth and perhaps not as well prepared as you could be.

The most important thing to recognize in these situ-ations is that you have choices. There are lots of bad choices you could make if you wanted to. You could run away. You could burst into tears. You could aban-don your presentation and have a meltdown. You could give in to the feeling that you are going to wet your-self and actually wet yourself. I have seen grown men do all these things at open-mic comedy nights. (OK, I haven't seen a grown man wet himself on stage. But there's still time. The American TV presenter Mel Rob-bins has talked extensively about wetting herself on stage in front of thousands of people during a keynote speech. These things happen. People style it out and don't die. Like I say, you have choices. First, congratu-late yourself on not making these bad choices. It's always comforting to realize that you haven't made a worse mistake. At least in *Sisters* the man did not have two ballerinas stuck up his bottom. Or three.)

In stand-up the interesting thing about the bad choices is that you tend not to see the 'running away' behaviour when people are being paid. And that's a significant point because it indicates that it's useful to ask the question: What's the professional thing to do here? What would an amateur do? What would a child do? What would a mature person do? What's tricky is that often you are being asked to respond in a professional manner to a situation that is unprofessional. It's unprofessional if someone interrupts you in a meeting. It's unprofessional if they openly steal your idea. In other situations, a colleague's behaviour might be transgressive, impolite or rude: it breaks with societal norms. (This is where extreme drunkenness in a comedy club might fit in.)

The concept known as 'happy high status' works well in a situation where things have gone wrong. This is a mode of being in which you are able to tolerate everything. It derives from the improvisation guru Keith Johnstone and the improv maxim 'Yes, and . . .' that I talked about in Chapter Five. The 'Yes, and . . .' idea is about accepting what the other person says and building on it. Its opposite is 'No, but . . .', where you negate the other person's behaviour and viewpoint and bring in a counterargument. 'No, but . . .' is the equivalent of the insect under the microscope fighting back. It might be your instinct to fight back and say: 'No, you don't get to interrupt me,' or 'No, you can't say that. That was my idea,' or 'No, you don't get to heckle me and be drunk during my time on stage. Get out.' But these things may not always be possible and they may not always be advisable. In a work situation, speaking your mind like this could get you sacked. (In some situations, though, it could be a great idea.) In comedy, it may turn the audience against you if they feel that you are being too harsh – and if they fear that you might then turn the same fire on them.

There is a combination of attitudes you can take here. Look for the mature thing to do. Look for the professional thing to do. Think to yourself: 'What's the "happy high status" response?' Think: 'How do I "Yes, and . . ." this behaviour? How do I accept it and build on it?' Make like the sisters in *Sisters*: accept what has happened and ask, 'What now?' When you mess up, the best next step is not necessarily easy but it is obvious. Diagnose honestly what happened without apportioning blame. That's for another day. Put your hands up to mistakes if it's safe to do so. Figure out the next thing that needs to happen. Accept what's behind you and move on. Not only will this usually allow you to 'climb' out of a hole with some dignity and integrity, but it also allows others to be lifted either by example or because you've helped rescue everyone from a mess or a big old blame party. No one wants to go to a blame party.

The benefit of 'outsider perspective'

There is a huge difference between the way most people operate at work and what I call 'outsider perspective' or 'freelancer mindset'. When you work in a collective, you're liable to think that not everything is your fault. (And you are sort of right.) When you work for yourself, you are forced to think that everything is your fault. (And you are sort of right.) I'm interested in finding a middle path between two these ways. Neither is quite true. One is too hands-off and lacks responsibility. And the other assumes too much responsibility. Generally speaking, people who work in groups need to take more personal responsibility for what's in their hands. And people who work for themselves need to ask for more help.

How have I come to think about these things? When I began performing stand-up around ten years ago, people started asking me to go into their workplaces to talk about everything from handling heckles and coping with rejection to the art of crowd control and turbo-boosting your creativity. I was surprised to find that I enjoyed talking about this stuff to people and handing over the small amount of initially fairly amateur, hard-won knowledge that I had. This morphed over time into performance coaching: I started seeing teams and individuals to talk to them about what they were struggling with and to find ways of fixing it.

Sometimes the 'performance' is literal: they need help with confidence, stagecraft, shaping a speech or handling nerves. Sometimes it is about their long-term work performance: how to manage colleagues better in meetings, how to plan their progression, how to structure their time. I have figured out how to do a lot of these things myself by doing them and 'failing up'. It can feel easier to 'fail' (usually a synonym for 'learning') and make mistakes when you work for yourself. We are more scared of failure when we are in a team and must answer to others.

What shocks me the most when I talk to people who don't work for themselves is how much they blame their colleagues and their bosses – anyone but themselves – for whatever isn't working out for them. If they don't get asked to do the presentations at work, they blame their boss or the colleague who always does it instead of initiating a conversation where they might offer an alternative way of doing things or where they might find out why they are being overlooked. If they are talked over in meetings, they blame the people who interrupt them instead of asking whether being in that meeting was the best way to achieve their goal, or instead of talking in advance to the person chairing the meeting to ask whether some time could be specifically ring-fenced for their idea. If they are overlooked for a promotion, they blame a pushy colleague instead of examining why it is that no one seems to know about all the things that they have achieved.

Of course, freelancers do this too. And many people give up freelancing because the responsibility and the rejection are hard to handle. As human beings, no matter what our chosen path, we love to blame other people. It's fun and it makes us feel good. If you have a bad comedy show or you do a speech that goes over as lukewarm, it feels good to say that the audience sucked and they didn't deserve you. If you don't get a pay rise or a promotion or someone copies your idea or is chosen over you, it feels good to say that everyone apart from you is a total moron. If someone criticizes something that you have written, it feels good to blame their bad taste. In some ways, we like paralysis because it means we don't have to do anything and we can enjoy the self-righteousness of complaining. And in some ways, we like criticism because it means we can run down the critic.

People who work on their own successfully have something to teach people who work in groups. When you work on your own, you don't have the luxury of complaining, largely because you don't have any colleagues to complain to. (Although I have recently acquired a cat for precisely this purpose. Hey, I am also human.) The truth is that there is no point in complaining because it won't help you move forward: you need to get on with people so that they will give you work.

Similarly, if criticism is constructive, you cannot afford to ignore it, because it will improve your work. And if you ignore it, you risk your work being of inferior quality and that is also going to prevent you from getting any more. Being able to absorb friction, take criticism and admit to failures and mistakes is all part of the job. If you can't manage those things, you don't last long as an independent.

Of course, none of us is perfect and lots of freelancers and entrepreneurs get these things wrong. But they can't go on getting them wrong, otherwise their business will fail. I see people in regular jobs indulging in blaming others on a long-term basis and there are no real consequences apart from their own ongoing misery. Provided their performance is adequate, they can continue in a job that is no fun to them at all. How to know if that's you? Be honest about how often you find yourself complaining about your circumstances. It can be hard to accept that others are unlikely to change and that the only person's behaviour you can change is your own. If you are unhappy, you are the one who needs to change something, whether it's looking for a new job, addressing a difficult issue or disciplining yourself to focus on the parts of your work you love rather than wallowing in the bits you hate.

My own mindset as a freelancer is that I'm prepared to court a lot of rejection in my work and I consider that the outcome of what I do is down to me and me alone.

That is true in all of the fields I've worked in: journalism, publishing, radio and TV work, and, more than anything, in stand-up comedy (where the audience is never to blame for how you come across – it's almost always your problem). You learn how to create opportunities for yourself in these fields. Be easy to work with. Be flexible. Be straightforward and honest wherever possible. Take on awkward conversations before things go wrong instead of afterwards. Admit your weaknesses (to yourself and others) and seek help in correcting them or in getting support in the areas where you don't excel. If you don't do this stuff as a freelancer, you tank.

The psychological lessons from the freelancer's mentality are, however, transferable across industries. Don't expect anyone to help you unless you help yourself. Make yourself indispensable by second-guessing what other people need and providing it for them before they know they need it. Go the extra mile. This mindset is also very easily summed up by that old saying: 'Do as you would be done by.' Even – perhaps especially – if no one else is doing that for you. I do realize how difficult it is to do this in a group work context. It's hard to take responsibility for mistakes because then others are liable to shift the blame on to you even more heavily and you can end up as the scapegoat for something that was a collective responsibility. There is a reason those boardroom moments on the TV show *The Apprentice* are so compelling: they're an illustration of people failing to take collective responsibility and instead choosing to identify who is personally liable. And that person gets fired. We all know that the person whose fault it really was may not necessarily get fired. It's all about how they massage the truth.

In real life we have the job of not behaving as if we're on *The Apprentice*, where the candidates do the opposite of Amy Poehler and Tina Fey in *Sisters*: instead of pulling together, they pull apart. This is not surprising because on *The Apprentice* there is one prize and only one person can win. In *Sisters*, they both risk going down and losing everything so their only option is to pull together. I would love it so much if one day on *The Apprentice*, they would all say, 'We lost this task jointly. You need to sack none of us or all of us.' The business of ducking responsibility and dodging bullets is all down to the failure to recognize that there is no one prize. In real life you do not win a large sum of money and a 'dream job' because you beat everyone else and proved that you were better than them. In real life you might have to work with those people again or you might have to ask one of them for a pay rise in a couple of years' time, or your 'dream job' might turn out to be not as advertised. In real life the roles of other people are key: they will only help you climb if you have demonstrated that you also lift others. None of us does any of this on our own. This is pragmatic as well as being the right thing to do. This part of lifting as you climb – making sure that you take personal responsibility for your fate – is the modern equivalent of the old saying: 'Be nice to people on the way up. Because you might meet them on the way down.'

CLIMB

● Be aware of how people you admire or respect handle failure, blame and making mistakes. In the environment you operate in, is it acceptable to say that you got something wrong? Context is really important and you have to be realistic. In some workplaces it might be unrealistic to be open about failures and you might have to save up practising that skill for a future job. It is worth asking the question: 'What happens here when things go wrong?' Because things always go wrong. And every environment needs a supportive system for dealing with that.

● Get comfortable with your deepest fears. Most people are stunned to find out that we all share the same basic 'secret' fears: rejection, loss, failure, humiliation, abandonment, death. None of these fears are personal to you, they're part of the human experience. In a situation where you fear making a mistake or failing, make a list of the worst things that could happen. ('I could get fired.' 'My reputation could be ruined.' 'I might offend someone.') Seeing your worst fears helps you to evaluate how likely they are to be realized. Next to the fear, write the next step. So beside 'I could get fired' write 'I would have to get another job.' Would that really be so bad? When we see through to the ultimate worst outcome, it's often surprisingly survivable. And in imagining it, we help ourselves to see just how unlikely it is. Merely thinking about these fears does not conquer them: you have to write them down. A list of five fears and five worst outcomes is a great place to start. And you might even surprise yourself at being unable to get to five. In spelling out our fears and articulating them, we can often see how irrational and impersonal they are.

● Glory in your noble failures. Keep a list of all the things you've done that went terribly wrong. Were there any upsides? There is often an unexpected upside to a mistake. It forced you to leave a job that didn't suit you. It avoided a bigger mistake. It made you realize you hadn't done enough research. A list of noble failures can help you to see that most 'mistakes' are just lessons to learn from. They are data.

● The Australian business coach Denise Duffield-Thomas advises regarding your biggest and most dramatic failures as material. One could be a chapter in a book or the title for a blog post. As she puts it, another could be the story you tell when you are interviewed by Oprah. The stories of our mistakes and failures are what make us interesting to others.

LIFT

● Lead by example by being open about your mistakes and failures. There's a balance to be had here: I'm not talking about putting a post on Instagram detailing 'Everything I Hate About Myself'. This topic works best when you can demonstrate what you learned and pass on that information to others so that they don't make the same mistake. Or so that they feel reassured about their own failures.

● Praise other people for admitting to mistakes and encourage a culture of learning and accountability. I know of one manager who gets team members to bake a homemade 'failure cake' – however poorly executed – to mark a project that has gone wrong. Everyone eats the cake as they discuss what happened and how it could be avoided again. You need to bake the cake yourself sometimes too. (We all do.)

● Share your story beyond your immediate environment. Almost all TED talks and good conference speeches are lessons in overcoming failure. We all want to be inspired and we all want to be given permission to mess up and not be judged. Spreading that message – whether it's a keynote, a blog post or a social media video – helps others feel less alone.

● In supporting other women, be a shoulder to cry on and stay in 'listening mode'. It can be really tempting when people get upset about failures and mistakes to rush straight to offering comfort: 'It doesn't matter.' 'It's a great lesson.' 'You'll get over it.' But people need to talk out their mistakes and their feelings of inadequacy before they can get to the lessons. Just as it's normal to make mistakes, it's also normal to feel crippling shame and immense idiocy. What's not right is staying in those feelings.

8

How to Support Other Women (without Disappearing Yourself)

'There is no limit to what we, as women, can accomplish.'
Michelle Obama

In the film *Mean Girls*, the young women who are the 'mean girls' are always drawing attention to themselves individually, each hoping to shine as the 'queen bee', but when it comes down to it they pass the buck and don't take responsibility. They're always ready to say, 'Oh, I don't know – Regina is the one who would know about that.' They don't want to be the leader. This is a natural teenage response. But it's apparent in grown women too. When they don't want to talk on a panel because they know someone else better qualified. (But I'm not asking her, I'm asking *you*.) When they don't want to be the one to ask for a pay rise because someone more senior should have that conversation and sort it for you. (Er, hello! I have been this person.) This is one of the few drawbacks of the idea of lifting as you climb. Some women use it as a way to 'hide'. Some women do everything they can to promote others and highlight the achievements of others and do nothing for themselves. 'Hiding' is defined as any activity that keeps you in the background, even if you seem to be very active. Hiding can include not taking up the opportunities that you're ready for – because something inside you tells you that you're 'not ready'. But even if you're not ready, it's only by doing it that you actually will be ready – remember the advice that you should never go for a job that you're already qualified to do. It's great to propose other women for things, but it's not right to push them forward as a way of hiding behind them. We need to know that we're 'lifting' for the right reasons and not because of our own insecurities.

The evidence that this 'hiding' plays out across the board is obvious to anyone who has ever tried to book a woman to speak at an event or on a panel or, generally, to anyone who has asked a woman to make herself more visible. I have worked on the periphery of radio and television for the best part of two decades, first as a journalist and as a guest on shows and later as a documentary-maker, presenter and playwright. I have also worked as a producer and a promoter of arts events and as the artistic director of a literature festival. I have booked many comedians and actors for events. I have asked hundreds of people to do things, maybe thousands. And I have a lot of friends who work in TV and radio production so I know I am not the only person who has observed this. Women love to find a reason to say no. Sometimes it's cosmetic and they want to say yes but they just want to make sure that you really want them. (I get that. We all have an ego.) Sometimes it's that they feel nervous about letting you down by underperforming and by agreeing only reluctantly they want to put that responsibility on you in case it doesn't work out: 'Well, you were the one who asked me . . .' But most of the time it is very simple. When someone asks a woman to do something visible, high-profile or challenging, it has become a female default for the woman to look behind her and say, 'Sorry, are you talking to me?' It's as if we think that someone has made a mistake to ask us and they must mean the other, more qualified, more confident, more accomplished invisible person who is standing behind us. It's the idea that somehow, somewhere, there is someone who is going to do this for us. That it's probably better and infinitely safer – to leave it up to them.

I have personally come full circle on this. I have been asked to do radio and TV appearances as a result of my writing since my early twenties and in my first job on a magazine. I would be asked to do terrible things. I realized much later that these requests were designed to fulfil the PR department's quota. They wanted to be able to boast about how many media appearances they had generated for the company. Their goal was quantity, not quality, and they didn't care whether the PR appearances were useful; they only cared that they were not especially damaging, and by putting up a low-level employee (me) who no one cared about they could achieve this goal. This is how I ended up appearing on television as an expert on 'car psychology'. I edited the motoring page on a men's magazine and although no person on earth is an actual 'car psychologist', the producers of the television programme were determined that this was what they wanted.

I appeared on live breakfast television opposite legendary presenter Dale Winton. My job was to explain why some people might want to buy a white car and some people might want to buy a black car. Somehow, I pulled this off without anyone jamming the channel's switchboard with complaints that everything I said was utter hogwash. (Learning point: no one cares about your stupid TV appearance, however stupid it is.) Pretending to be a car psychologist was one of the weirdest jobs I've ever had. But it was also one of the most enjoyable. Heavily made up and wearing a fixed grin, I was plonked in a car park in Isleworth next to a mahogany-hued Dale, who took urgent puffs on his cigarette between live takes. He had an assistant dedicated to holding his cigarette off-camera. (A second learning point: nothing is ever as it seems.)

Despite realizing that the car-psychologist episode had been a waste of my time, I continued to allow my arm to be twisted by the magazine's desperate PR team. Later, as a result of being the editor of the health pages, I ended up talking about penis-enlargement surgery on the daytime TV staple *Richard & Judy*. The magazine I was working on ran a lot of articles on this topic so I did at least know a little more about penile enhancement than I knew about the psychological effects of car colours. My default at this point in my career was to say yes to everything and to count it all as good experience. It was foolish. But I was young.

The principle of saying yes to everything is not a bad mentality to have. You can use the experience as an information-gathering exercise – although it would of course be better to have the opportunity to discuss subjects you actually know something about. Doing things when you're not really ready for them is good as long as it doesn't harm your reputation. You can learn a lot. That no one cares what you say on television (as long as you don't create a meme or a GIF), they only care what you look like. That enough TV make-up can make us all look attractive. That television (and many speaking experiences) are not about actually knowing anything, they are about being able to look as if you know something.

I do have sympathy for people who say no to things rather than yes. Some things really are a waste of time. And there are opportunities you might be offered where you really are out of your depth. What matters most is to work this out: what is the benefit of saying yes? And what is the cost of saying no? If you are clear on this, it's an easy decision.

When are you saying no for the right reasons? And when are you hiding?

There are a lot of women who say yes for the right reasons and lean into whatever sound and meaningful opportunities they are offered. But there are plenty who don't respond in that way. If you have ever hesitated to say yes to something that scares you, then you are not alone. After I stopped trying to please the magazine's PR department, whenever I was asked to do something exciting or challenging that represented a step up in my work, I would immediately think of other people (especially women) who 'deserved' it more than I did or who would be better at doing it than me. It's easy to bat away requests, saying, 'No, thank you, I'm not the right person to ask. Have you thought about so-and-so?' The problem is that you then, from afar, have to watch the other person doing that job with a little pang of regret in your heart, but also, very probably, a slight feeling of smugness that you have orchestrated some good in the world. This is a really awkward moment. It's great to do things for other people. It's great to recommend other people for things when you are too busy or it's really not quite right or you've already done that thing and you're now bored of it. But it is not right to facilitate the advancement of others at your own expense. The good feelings will last for a while. But they will very quickly turn to resentment. And we must all do everything we can to avoid fostering resentment in our lives. Because a resentful person can neither climb nor lift. In my experience – because I have been this person – all they can do is eat a lot of biscuits.

One of the biggest challenges of moving forward, taking up leadership roles or doing anything where you are asking other people to invest in you or believe in you is that, by necessity, it involves asserting yourself over others. This can be a very difficult bind. I was recently asked to interview an author on stage for a large sum of money. I was happy to do it and really wanted to do it. But I also knew another interviewer (a woman) who had a close relationship with this author and might feel that she should have been offered this opportunity over me. (And she would probably be right.) If I didn't know this interviewer, it wouldn't matter. But I do and she's a friend. So the only right thing for me to do was to message her and say: 'I've been offered this thing. I want to do it – but I think they should have asked you. Would you want to do it? Are you free to do it?' My friend wasn't free to do it so I said yes. And I knew that I'd done the right thing.

But it's also possible to see my response as controlling. It shouldn't be necessary to rule out every single other person who would be right for a job before you can feel OK about saying yes. We forget sometimes that if someone asks you to do something, you do them a courtesy by proving them right in their choice. Supposing someone asks you to do something and you laugh in their face and say, 'Who? Me? Are you kidding? There are loads of people better qualified than I am.' You are insulting that person's professionalism. They contacted *you*. It's worth remembering that it is a great privilege to be asked, to be chosen.

It's impossible to know for certain whether women turn things down more often than men, but there seems to be a lot of evidence that they do. There are not as many opportunities for women and so we know that when we are offered something it's unusual. This is a fact. The evidence is replicated across hundreds of industries: I recently read of a woman who works in architecture talking about having asked forty-eight women to appear on panels. Eighteen said yes. That is a pathetic strike rate. And it's incredibly stressful and demotivating for the people organizing events. To have to ask three times as many women in order to get a yes? That's exhausting. It's enough to make you give up and just ask more men. Which is, of course, why this problem exists.

Once we get ourselves into a secure enough position – as an industry expert, as an experienced contributor, as a representative of a cause – we might then be able to say no to an offer in order to create an opportunity for another woman. It's OK to say no as long as it's not because we are scared or we want to hide behind someone else's contribution, but because we genuinely don't need the opportunity and we know that someone else would benefit from it. In terms of how you relate to the rest of the human race, this feeling is a good one. It's empathy. It's gratitude. It's about 'checking your privilege'. Being aware that, although life is not a zero-sum game, when you are offered something, there is someone who has not been offered that thing. Finding a way around this without explicitly disadvantaging yourself, or 'virtue-signalling' in order to make yourself look more saintly or by patronizing others, is hard. But it's an important challenge to take on. It's also a great reason to start taking up – and creating – opportunities for yourself in the short term. You can think, 'I know I'm not ready for this but I'm going to do it to show other women that you don't have to be 100 per cent ready to do these things.' You can do it imperfectly and you can learn on the job. And you can think, 'I'm going to promise myself that I will get five opportunities under my belt. And then I will offer one to one of my junior colleagues.' You can make that offer in a way that is not patronizing and so that person never finds out that they weren't the first choice. Or you can be direct and say, 'I can't do this next panel appearance. Do you want to do it? I think you're ready.'

185

And if they say, 'Oh no, I'm not ready,' you can say, 'I thought that too when I started. The time to start is before you're ready.'

How to create opportunities for everyone

One of the great tricks of creating opportunities for yourself is to think about how that initiative could better others further down the line. This works particularly well if you are feeling nervous about something. It's amazing how easily these feelings are activated. I recently set up a dinner with a new friend. We wanted to invite about twenty women we didn't know very well to a networking event. We did it in a spirit of experimentation as we were both fed up of going to events where we didn't know anyone and there was no meaningful conversation. It was something we really wanted to do and we knew it would be fun. I had an inkling that if we did it, other people might see that they too have permission to do this. It's one antidote to women feeling alone in what they do. And it's a way of networking without it being a cringe.

But we began to tie ourselves up in knots. Could we use the word 'networking'? Would people be put off by that? Would people think we were trying to bring them together for some unexplained purpose? Would we look as if we had an agenda? Would people be OK about paying for their own dinner or would they expect us to pay for it? Eventually I got sick of asking myself these questions and focused on the fact that people know their own minds. If they like the idea of it, they'll see it as an opportunity. If they don't, they can say they're busy that night. We were up front with exactly what our intentions were. We were clear about the fact that everyone would be paying their own way. And we explained that it was an experiment. The word 'experiment' is so useful and we don't use it anything like enough. You can get away with anything if you call it an experiment. It's the perfect get-out-of-jail-free card, where you have a built-in possibility for failure and it doesn't matter because it was an experiment. In the end everyone who came said they wanted to do something similar.

Going out on a limb and creating something that doesn't already exist – and being straightforward about why you're trying it and how it's OK if it doesn't work – is extremely powerful. And it encourages other people to try things. One of the only ways for us all to bust out of the negative statistics about female representation is to put ourselves up for more things, have other people see us getting rejected and not being destroyed by it. It's not always easy to keep your morale up, especially if you are going after things that are difficult or that haven't been attempted before. But it really helps to play a mind trick on yourself where you de-personalize it and think, 'I'll put myself up for this. And if I get rejected, then maybe the next woman will get accepted.' Not every yes has to be for you. And someone else might have got a no so that you could get a yes. We all have to expose ourselves to the possibility of 'no' more often. As mentioned previously – because I can't say it often enough – remember that 'No' often means 'Not right now,' or 'Almost – try again with a different idea.'

CLIMB

● Think about where you stand in relation to the idea of 'say yes to everything'. There are many contradictory ways of looking at this and your attitude to it depends on what you want to achieve at any given time. If you are in a rut and want to shake things up, saying yes to things that scare you is useful. So you should make a list called something like 'Things I Would Say Yes To If I Wasn't Scared'. If, however, you are going through a period where you're overwhelmed and over-scheduled, you need to reprioritize. Your list might be: 'What I Should Be Saying No To'. The trick is to define when you are wasting energy and when you are 'hiding'.

● If you find yourself saying no to opportunities a lot – or passing them on to other women – then ask yourself why you do this. Is it because you genuinely don't want the opportunities? Or because you are scared of how you will be judged? Not everyone wants to be a great public speaker or represent their company on television. But is this holding you back? Will this attitude cause you to miss out on future opportunities?

● Ask for help. Ask a boss or a colleague or a mentor to ask you for proof that you've been putting yourself forward for things. Ask them to call you out when they see you passing the buck.

• Ask for extra training, support, tuition, coaching – whatever you need – to develop the skills you need. This is an investment in you and many companies have money set aside for this investment. You do need to investigate and ask for it. Do not expect it to land in your lap. A senior woman told me recently that she was amazed when she was promoted and discovered that all the people at that level (up until then, all men) had a dedicated PR at their disposal to help them with self-promotion and media visibility. She realized too late that she could have asked for it much earlier but no one had told her this opportunity existed.

LIFT

• Find ways to encourage other women who you think might be 'hiding'. Devise ways in which it is safe for them to fail. Facilitate training, workshops, networks where they can practise things in a safe environment. In some companies, there is a weekly chance for one person or a number of people to give a progress report or an update about what has happened that week: wins, lessons, new clients, nuggets of news that not everyone might have picked up on. It can be really informal, no pressure. Creating low-level, no-big-deal speaking opportunities is a way to get practice without anyone feeling too vulnerable.

● Make time to give individual feedback to people you work with. A lot of the time we hide behind others because no one has told us what our qualities are or what makes us special. Lots of people have no idea what exactly is keeping them in their place of work other than the fact that they 'haven't been found out yet'. If you can articulate and define what people's strengths are and praise them openly, they will play to those strengths.

● Be a role model for vulnerability and failure. (This is challenging!) Show younger and less experienced members of your team that you have failed and sur-vived, that you go into situations sometimes not knowing what you're doing and it works out OK. Look for opportunities to 'model' (showcase or spotlight) resilience. If they see that you can cope in the face of difficulty whilst not being perfect and all-knowing, they will believe they can do it too.

9

How to Handle Rivalry

*'Girls compete with each other.
Women empower one another.'*
Fridge magnet

In the 1950 film *All About Eve*, Bette Davis plays Margo
Channing, a wonderfully diva-ish actress who has had
a rather charmed life and career. She appears to have
achieved all her goals, to have fulfilled all her ambitions, and is simply enjoying the continuation of her
fabulousness. It goes without saying that she has excellent hair. Margo is faintly aware that she's ageing. But
she doesn't need to think about that too much as her
career is going so marvellously. No surprise, then, that
a fangirl, Eve Harrington (played by Anne Baxter in the
film), a sweet young woman with her own acting ambitions, wants to be Margo's assistant. Immediately any
onlooker can see what is going to happen. Eve is the
cuckoo in the nest. She's going to copy Margo, cosy up
to her contacts, exploit her connections and use her
new mentor to further her own career, all under the
guise of friendship and support. As Margo begins to

become paranoid about what's going on (although it's hardly paranoia, as she's right . . .), she says the immortal line: 'Fasten your seatbelts. It's going to be a bumpy night.'

This is a statement of war. Margo is not going down without a fight. The problem is, we know that she's doomed. Unless she can make a new path for herself, one which allows there to be a way forward for her but also room for Eve, she is going to be the one who loses out. And we know that Margo is not going to be able to formulate this plan because she is too self-centred. If she can't 'win', then she won't want to be in the game at all. And she certainly won't be able to share with Eve, let alone do anything that might actively promote the younger woman. Margo is not able to lift and so she has to stop climbing altogether. Eve, meanwhile, climbs over everyone to get where she wants. In an inevitable but beautiful twist at the end of the film, when Eve has triumphed, she comes back to her room to find her own 'Eve' waiting for her. A young student called Phoebe – a fan – has broken into her apartment. A final scene sees Phoebe trying on Eve's dress and imagining herself collecting an award. Someone else, it seems, is always waiting in the wings. Climb as high as you want, someone else is always coming up the ladder behind you.

This doesn't have to be a female story. After all, men fight each other for accolades all the time. But it's hard to imagine a version of *All About Eve* in which Margo and Eve are replaced by Malcolm and Euan. (Personally, I would not rush to see *All About Euan*.) The quality of collusion and intimacy is completely different for women. It has never been socially acceptable for us to be open rivals to each other. We are expected to be 'sisterly'. *All About Eve* is a fantastically compelling story because it reveals women being transgressive and doing what they are not supposed to do: put one over on each other. Even more brilliantly, this is not like Alexis Colby and Krystle Carrington in the 1980s TV show *Dynasty,* where they are overtly sworn rivals and ready for a shoulder-padded catfight at any moment. This is a more spidery, less camp version of quiet, deadly female competition. Where one minute it seems as if you have found a delightful new friend and companion, and the next you realize that she wants to kill you and eat you. It taps into a primal fear about women and ambition: that women can only get what they want by destroying other women's opportunities.

Things have moved on since Bette Davis first uttered the line: 'I'll admit I may have seen better days, but I'm still not to be had for the price of a cocktail, like a salted peanut.' The story in *All About Eve* – of a younger woman coming up behind an older woman and 'stealing' her spot – is, ridiculously, still playing itself out in our collective subconscious. The reaction to the recent theatre remake of *All About Eve*, starring Gillian Anderson as

Margo and Lily James as Eve, was interesting, as a lot of people complained that Gillian Anderson was too young and beautiful to be believable in the role. This, even though Gillian Anderson was almost a decade older than Bette Davis when she played Margo. (Anderson was fifty; Davis was forty-two. Anne Baxter was twenty-seven; Lily James was twenty-nine.) Our attitudes have moved on: we are more resistant to believing that an older woman will be ousted just because of her age. But it's fascinating that no one complained that the rivalry wouldn't exist and a young woman wouldn't behave that way. That wasn't questioned. That was still a given. Audiences just thought that Eve's quest would be a little bit more difficult to achieve because her rival wasn't *that* old. They didn't believe that women had become any more collaborative or any less likely to claw each other's eyes out. It's that piece that we need to fix. The day when someone watches *All About Eve* and says, 'But why would women behave like that towards each other? What a dated idea!' is the moment when we will have made progress.

Do any of us really need rivals?

There is still a fear amongst women that this kind of rivalry exists. From the perspective of ageism, there is, of course, some evidence that it is real, less because of the dynamic between women and more because of society's obsession with youth; we are all aware that there are many situations in life where we are liable to be replaced by a younger, 'better' model of ourselves. The *All About Eve* paradigm is less about ageism than it is about female rivalry: the 'other woman' doesn't have to be younger. She can be fresher, newer, more exciting, different. The lure of the new is just as powerful as the threat of the young. The Eve character simply represents a woman who resembles us closely enough to be a threat. The sting in the tail is the connection between the two rivals: as in the film *Single White Female*, there's an element of admiration and worship which is intertwined with the urge to destroy or 'win' in the most complicated way. (Let's not dwell on *Single White Female*, though, as it's really a homicidal 1990s version of *All About Eve* featuring a clear case of narcissistic personality disorder.)

I think the 'ageism' aspect to this unsisterly usurping is receding. It's common now – thank goodness – to hear countless reports of older women feeling energized and getting a new lease of life for all sorts of reasons (from children leaving home to coming out the other side of the menopause). I love nothing better than to read stories of women who have started businesses in their sixties or seventies or become a supermodel at the age of ninety-seven. (Thank you, Iris Apfel.) This would not have been the case when 1950s audiences were watching *All About Eve*. But alongside the evidence that we live in an increasingly ageless society, there are also the stories of older women who feel sidelined, who feel that they weren't able to achieve their ambitions in a chosen field once they got to a certain age. Maybe they started another business because, just as they felt they were getting somewhere, too many Eve characters came along.

All this is compounded by tensions around digital media and the fact that anyone over the age of thirty-five has grown up in a completely different digital universe. (I'm not saying these things can't be learned at any age but there is a marked generational differ-ence here and it plays out in all sorts of complicated ways.) On the flip side of that, younger women fre-quently complain that they want to be taken seriously and listened to, and the first things I am asked in per-formance workshops with tech companies (who tend to have younger employees) are 'How can I make myself seem older? How can I get more gravitas?' This always makes me laugh. Older colleagues want to appear young, fresh and up to date. The younger ones want to appear old and wise. Everyone feels that they have to pretend to be something that they're not, when often the attributes that we need are present already. So how can you have the grace of Bette Davis's Margo Channing whilst not having to step aside for Anne Baxter's Eve Harrington? What would it look like if the two of them just got on and helped each other?

What if there were no bumpy night for anyone and we could all just get in the same car and have a very nice trip out with everyone getting what they wanted?

We need to look at age and generational differences with an open mind and with brutal honesty. We need to share information and insights. I recently had a conversation with a younger colleague that made me really uncomfortable, but afterwards I was glad it happened because I could tell it had helped her. I was telling her that, now that I'm in my forties, I had suddenly realized the truth about a lot of the work I was asked to do in my twenties and thirties. I thought I was asked to do the work because I was good at it. And hopefully that was part of the reason I was asked. But, I now realize, it was only part of the reason. Looking back, I can see now that I was asked to do some of it because my face fitted: I was the right age, I had just about the right experience, I was available for the right price. My competence was useful, but it was incidental. I wouldn't have been asked to do it if I were twenty years older. And I certainly wouldn't have been asked to do it if I had asked for more money. (Although it's possible I could have leveraged my work much more powerfully if I had known how to negotiate at a younger age.) I could see the colour drain out of my younger friend's face as I told her this. 'What can anyone do to avoid this?' she asked. The only answer is that it would be wise not to have too many illusions about yourself.

We all know that in different industries there are times in life when you are particularly likely to shine. This is really obvious in some professions, like sport or dance. And there's a whole support system for some people which acknowledges that you have to reinvent yourself at a certain age because your career can't continue. In other jobs, though, it's hard to shine for thirty or forty years non-stop. And yet we are all trying to run careers that may have to last for up to fifty years. This all makes it even more important for women to support each other and to try to combat some of this rivalry and ageism stuff. Eve does not have to oust Margo to succeed. Why can't they be in a play together? Or why can't Eve write a play for Margo, or vice versa?

How to keep a level head about the competition

One of the most useful responses to incidents of people encroaching on your territory – and I am talking about incidents both real and imagined (and they are, I think, often imagined) – is a Madonna quote from years ago: 'There are enough crowns for us all to be queens.' This has recently been repurposed into an Instagram meme which has featured prominently in Miss Universe speeches: 'Real queens fix each other's crowns.' This motto goes to the heart of the issue of female ambition being mistaken for bitchy female rivalry. It's tempting to imagine the contestants back-stage at Miss Universe pouring glue into each other's mascara wands and ripping each other's hair extensions out, because that is a better story than giving them the benefit of the doubt. None of us want to be self-righteous goodie-goodies who are pretending that we only do things for other women, that we don't want anything another woman has and 'Don't give me the crown, she deserves it more.' Please! But we need to get past the push-pull of the drama of this concept. It doesn't have to be Margo versus Eve. And it doesn't have to be The Margo and Eve Sorority Foundation. It can be something creative in between.

A great way to get around this would be to embrace sensible, level-headed disagreement in public without turning it into a slanging match. There's a public narrative that plays out in the media and also in workplaces that when two women disagree everyone turns to each other metaphorically and whispers: 'Catfight!' As a result, women can often be afraid to disagree with each other publicly, even if they have opposing views. It's also true that audiences struggle to watch women expressing opposing views.

I once got myself into some avoidable trouble on stage at a panel event by voicing a thought that was going through my head but would have been – perhaps – better left unsaid: 'There's nothing more boring than a load of women on stage agreeing with each other.' It wasn't a criticism of the event I was participating in at the time. It was a defence: I was arguing (gently) with a point that someone else had made. And everyone was looking at me, horrified, as if to say: 'You are supposed to be a nice woman. Why are you disagreeing, however gently?' I take the opposite view. If you've been asked to speak in front of people, it's because you should have something to say that makes them think. It needs to be interesting, well thought through, insightful, evidenced, entertaining. Any or all of these things. What it should not be is the equivalent of saying: 'I think the same thing as what the last person said.' (Disclaimer: it is OK to say this if you are caught out because you have no knowledge of a subject or no genuine opinion. But generally try to avoid situations where you could be caught out or asked to speak about something about which you have no knowledge or strong opinions.)

You may, like me, have attended work events – panels, conferences, debates, broadcast moments – where the women involved seem to shy away from disagreeing with each other, in however minor a way. I hate drawing this gender distinction. But I have to be honest and say that I've seen it many times. Sometimes it's to do with casting: it's not always easy to find a selection of people who hold opinions which are different enough to each other. Sometimes the people who are booking speakers for a panel have all kinds of considerations: they want famous people or they want 'the person of the moment' or they have to include someone who is a friend of so-and-so. This happens. And you might be there because you are a friend of so-and-so. Or because your boss pulled out and they've dropped you in it. But you have to try to rise to the occasion and find something interesting to say. Not unnecessarily and falsely provocative. But what you really think.

The result of this is that the only women we see disagreeing publicly are women with extreme views, who often seem to be saying things for the sake of being controversial. (This is not a gendered activity. Many men also make this the hallmark of their debate style: just say the most outrageous thing and troll everyone.) I'd like to see more women with nuanced but varying views politely but robustly disagreeing with each other. More of us need to be prepared to do this – and be ready to accept it when others criticize us for our views. It's not personal and it's not because they're trying to break into your dressing room to try on your favourite gown and take a selfie of themselves with your Academy Award. It's just that they disagree with you. Which is normal. In my experience, women do tend towards agreement and backing each other's arguments up, perhaps because we are programmed to be collegiate or because we don't want to be 'disliked' by onlookers. And there are times when offering each other support is the right thing to do. The reality is that it's incredibly boring to watch people on a panel agree and back each other up. This doesn't mean that the only alternative is to tear each other apart or aggressively break down the other person's arguments. Again, this is about having the guts to experiment and find the middle ground. Not only for ourselves or because it's the right thing to do. But because if other women see you doing it, then they too will be emboldened to do it.

CLIMB

• The way to avoid becoming obsessed with your 'rivals' is to cultivate a healthy attitude towards envy. Eve envies Margo and so she aims to take what Margo has. Instead she could have just made a 'Useful Envy List' and turned it into a mission. Envy is helpful because it pinpoints what is missing from our own lives. How can you get some of what that person has? How can you use their success to inspire you? What exactly is it that this person has that you want? Is it realistic for you to aim for that thing? Is it healthy?

• Whenever you do sense rivalry or envy, be creative in your thinking and make sure you know the full picture. There is no point envying someone their work success only to later find out that they are a regular cocaine user. (This happened to me. That is, I envied someone their success. I was not the cocaine user.) Be careful you are not wasting negative energy on pointless targets.

• If you sense that someone else is attempting to become a rival to you, one solution is to be generous and open-hearted. It's a compliment, after all. We all have moments of insecurity and weakness. We all get crazy ideas. Sometimes you might be in the path of it. Just let it play out and try to stay out of the way.

• If you have a genuine situation (confirmed by other colleagues or friends and not just the voice in your head) with someone who is actively undermining you, seek help. Talk discreetly to other colleagues or to a boss. See what can be done without making the other person feel small and without making you look petty. If the situation persists and no one is taking action, can you get out or move sideways? Life is too short to waste on toxic people.

• There is a lot of weird rivalry and competition on social media and some of it is painfully obvious. Try to develop your own attitude to how you approach and support others on social media and what you expect in return. Do not get hung up on who is retweeting who or who is following who. Be secure in your own decisions and your own way of working. Do not expect others to do favours for you but give favours freely if you can afford to. Ask yourself: 'Am I being the bigger person here?' Always try to be the bigger person. (Without ever telling anyone this, as that is very much not the bigger-person thing to do.)

LIFT

• If you are in the position to help someone who could become a rival, nip any feelings of competition in the bud by befriending them. As Simon Sinek explores in his book *The Infinite Game*, you are much more likely to benefit yourself and become a happier person long term if you are an ally to people who could be seen as rivals. Often these people can help you find your own points of difference and cement your niche. In turn, if you help them find their point of difference, they are likely to support you in return. This stuff is nuanced and needs to be explored discreetly and over the long term. I am not talking about contacting them and saying, 'We're obviously rivals but let's work together.' This is maybe a little too direct.

● Look out for colleagues who are getting caught up in pettiness and pointless competition and gently help them to defuse situations or take the heat out of things. Do not be the one who adds fuel to the fire. Do not be the person who encourages drama.

● Be the person who does the unexpected thing. Maybe Margo Channing might have defused some of Eve Harrington's envy if she had introduced her to an agent immediately. Make introductions, make connections, share contacts, be open to possibilities. Let these things take on a life of their own.

10

How to Reach Out for Help (Elegantly), Especially When You Fear Rejection

> *'It's never overreacting to ask for what
> you want and need.'*
> Amy Poehler

The actress Melissa McCarthy strikes me as a very 'lift as you climb' kind of person. She trained as an improviser and the motto that many improvisers use before they go on stage (with no script and no rehearsal) is: 'I've got your back.' In the on-screen role of Lee Israel in *Can You Ever Forgive Me?*, however, she plays the part of someone who desperately needs to be lifted but does not know how to ask for that help – and shuns anyone who tries to give it to her.

The film portrays the real-life story of Israel, who gets trapped in a scam of her own making. Israel is plagued by financial difficulties and alcoholism. Her biography of the actress Fanny Brice is a failure. In desperation, Israel tries to sell some of Brice's letters, only to be told that they are 'boring'. She realizes that if she can copy the handwriting and write something witty at the end, they will sell for more money. She then becomes caught up in creating other forgeries. They are beautiful. But the scam has to unravel at some point and she knows it's only a matter of time. Over a number of years Israel has moments when she could ask her boss, her agent, her bookseller, her ex-girlfriend . . . But she just can't do it. She cannot say the words 'I need help,' even to other women – which is perhaps the biggest tragedy of all – and so she becomes utterly lost and isolated.

Melissa McCarthy portrays this state brilliantly, managing to make Israel into a desperate, desolate figure whilst still encouraging us to feel empathy for her rather than disgust. It is very easy – tempting, even – to think that you can manage things on your own and that if you found your way into this mess it must be possible to find your way out. And won't other people only complicate things? The film becomes much less about Israel's personal situation and much more about a universal problem: getting trapped in our own narrative of heroic victimhood. 'I'm fine. I don't need anyone's help, thank you very much.'

I see lots of women experiencing this at work. Either they get sucked into the trap of constantly moaning and bitching with colleagues about some awful situation without anyone ever seeking to find a solution, or they become the isolated martyr, almost proud of their own ability to survive without having to admit weakness to anyone. The first option – 'Let's go for Friday-night drinks every week and complain for four hours about our boss without anyone actually challenging the boss's behaviour' – is unhelpful. But this method at least has the comfort of being collegiate. You may not be changing your situation in any meaningful way but at least you're making work friends. Misery loves company. And friendship based on that kind of adversity can last for ever. The other method is just you on your own, stewing in your own juices, going round in circles, patting yourself on the back for your self-sufficiency. True, you are unlikely to end up being investigated by the FBI for your shameless forgeries of 'lost' Dorothy Parker letters. But you are liable to end up in just as lonely a place as the Lee Israel portrayed in the film.

Our inability to ask for support is toxic to us, especially when other people love to help. This is the terrible irony of the 'lonely furrow' scenario. Whilst you may think it is excruciating to ask for things or show weakness or explicitly request help, when the situation is the other way round we find it extraordinarily gratifying to be asked for help. Whenever you are thinking that you hate asking for help, remember how much you like giving it. Being asked for help makes us feel needed, powerful, authoritative, wanted, vital. Why wouldn't you want to make someone else feel like that? It's a great gift.

This is a dynamic that is replicated in a common attitude to public speaking or appearing in front of other people. When we consider doing this, we really don't want to fail or mess up or forget things or fall over or discover that our shirt has dropped open revealing our bra. But when we see this happen to other people, we love it. And I don't mean in a nasty way. When we are in the audience we are extremely forgiving of people when things go wrong. We like it. It shows that it's live. It shows that the other person is human. It shows that it's possible to recover from mistakes. It makes you feel relieved that you are not the one up there going through that.

One of the best early shows I ever did as a stand-up comedian was marked by an audience response I had never experienced before: they were totally on my side from the very first second. I felt as if I could have said anything and it would be funny. I didn't need to do a thing. I realized later on that my bra was showing through my top for the entire show. I was ashamed and embarrassed. But actually it had done me a favour. I was unwittingly humble and that had made it funnier. (You can't replicate this, of course. These things are only funny if they happen by accident. I do not advise you to invest in a wardrobe of see-through tops. For me, maybe that's an act for a future incarnation.)

Asking for help is like messing up on stage: it's an admission that you are a human being. What is so scary about that? On the contrary, it's a wonderful thing and other people will appreciate you for it. Giving other people the chance to be kind, generous, open and giving, whether it's in support as an audience or by assisting with something that you need in your work or your life – that is a great thing to do. We should not be afraid of it. We should embrace it.

How to not ask for help in an annoying way

Of course, there's a fine line here. You have to need the help. You can't be wimping out at the slightest thing or expecting other people to do things for you. Something a lot of young people seem to do is to write a sob story on social media about how lousy their situation is and how terrible their life is and how if you don't help them with a job now, they won't be able to pay their rent. I'm not sure this scattergun approach is classy. If it yields results, I'm happy to stand corrected. Sometimes, desperate times call for desperate measures. But it would be nice to be able to ask for help – possibly offline and in person – before you get to the point where you have to write a status update which says, 'Please give me work.'

Part of the problem with these open appeals for help is that they suggest you have no discretion. If you are writing about your problem on social media, how does the person who helps you know that you won't write about their help in the same way? Not everyone feels comfortable with everyone knowing who they've 'helped' and why. These things are sensitive and personal. It's always worth stepping outside of yourself and thinking, 'How would I feel if I saw this? Would I give someone work if I saw them asking for it in this way?' If you feel hesitant, try another way.

It's much better to find realistic sources of help and send them personalized, targeted approaches. Or talk to them in person. An appeal for help is pointless unless it stands a chance of success. Some of the more modern ways of asking for help are a way for you to pretend to yourself that you are doing something ('I put it on my Facebook!') without you actually doing something that will yield a result. You'll get the same advice from anyone who knows anything about job searches. Best to start with people who know you and widen the search from there than to send your CV to 500 random companies.

This is the key to asking for anything and making sure you get it: know what you want. When you are asking for help, the more specific you can be, the better. I have mentioned the importance of being succinct and specific before. It focuses people, it makes them feel special and it makes it harder to say no. I was once approached by a distant acquaintance in dire straits who asked me if I could give them £50,000. (I don't even want to think about why they thought I had £50,000 lying about the place.) I felt that it would be mean to ignore this request so I replied. Probably a mistake. I said I was very sorry but I did not have access to this kind of money and I hoped they found a solution to their problem. Another reply came swiftly, 'OK, if you don't have £50,000, do you have £50?' I'm not joking. At this point I felt angry. This way of requesting help was such a waste of time and was only going to result in the person on the receiving end saying no. If, however, they had sent me a link to a Kickstarter with a suggested donation, then I might have felt ready to help and less like I was being scammed.

You also need to not be what people have started calling an 'askhole'. The askhole comes in many forms but there are two common types. There are askholes who ask for advice and then ignore it (and let you know that they ignored it). And there are askholes who ask for a specific thing, you give it to them and then they say, 'Oh, it's OK, I don't need it now anyway.' When you ask for help, you need to be sure that this is the help that you need and you need to be willing to accept the help when it is offered to you. Don't be asking for help if you're going to change your mind halfway through. Naturally, sometimes people will give you help that turns out to be the wrong help. Or they will give you advice that makes you think, 'I would rather boil my head than do that.' But you need to keep those things to yourself and be gracious. Ask graciously and straightforwardly. And receive the help graciously and straightforwardly.

How do you ask for help with grace? And how do you recognize when other women need help – and offer it in a way that is easy to accept?

Something strange can happen when women reach out to each other for help. It's to do with well-meaning desperation, or perhaps it's misplaced chutzpah. But if the answer is no, for whatever reason, the person in need sometimes says, 'But you owe this to me because you are a woman and you should support other women.' I think of it as 'I'm Entitled to Your Help' syndrome.

It is now fashionable to champion sisterhood and channel some of the ideas brought up by the #MeToo movement into collective action. We've also seen the rise of political entities like the Women's Equality Party in the UK. That's all great. If these things appeal to you, this kind of collective action can be incredibly inspiring and supportive. We need people who can lend their energy and dynamism to these causes. But the existence of all these things does not mean that other women were put here to help you. Collective action is very different to an individual ask. Just because the #MeToo movement exists and is a legitimate expression of sisterhood, it doesn't mean that you have to undertake a six-hour round trip to a conference to talk about women's empowerment for no money. (In fact, it probably means the opposite: the more we talk about

feminism, sisterhood and overturning patriarchal attitudes, the more we should stand up for ourselves and
make sure our time is valued, our expertise is acknow-
ledged and our efforts properly remunerated.)

Frequently, if I turn things down, there is pushback.
'Don't you want to be an example to other women?' I've
also had this response: 'You are always encouraging
people to invite women on to panels. And yet you don't
want to do this one.' The inference here is: 'You can't
say no to us even if we are asking you to speak on a subject you are not interested in on a day when you are
not free.' It's similarly awkward if the financials of an
arrangement cannot be worked out to mutual benefit. Sometimes people think I ought to do an event for
free and I disagree. This is a huge trap for women: I've
often got into conversations with people where they've
asked if they can invite me to something and I've said,
of course, anyone is welcome to invite me to anything.
(Me, inwardly: 'Doesn't mean I'll say yes.') But the
assumption from that response means not only that I
have already said yes but that I have agreed to do some
kind of work at this event for nothing. Say what? This is
where we get so obsessed with the idea of sisterhood
('She must want to help us out!') that we don't respect
boundaries or professionalism.

We've all asked for favours we shouldn't have asked
for. We've all sent emails that were too long and too
needy. We've all pestered people a bit more than we

should have. It's OK. No one is perfect all the time. But we need to recognize that it's wrong and try to be judicious about how we approach others and how we ask for help. You need to think about how someone is going to receive your request. And you need to make it easy for them to say yes. Be sure to ask them for something that is in their gift to give and makes them feel good. Set a deadline for their response. Be relaxed about them saying no. Depersonalize it: you are asking for a specific kind of support or assistance; you are not asking for their general approval of you as a human being.

CLIMB

● One of the best lessons I've ever learned in work – and it applies in public speaking too – is to ask for what you want. In work this means figuring out what you're asking for: a specific sum of money, a specific task, a specific commitment on a specific day. Be as direct and straightforward as possible. If you're putting your request in an email, get to it within three to five sentences. If you're saying it face to face, get to it within five minutes. I've sat through two-hour meetings when I've eventually asked for what I want at the end and the other person has said, 'Oh, I can't make that decision. You're asking the wrong person.' Say at the start, 'Let me tell you up front what I'm looking for at the moment.'

● It is possible to ask other people for help in any situation, as long as you leave room for them to say no. You don't need to put up with a situation you're finding difficult. If you're giving a speech and you hate the way the stage is set up, ask for help getting it changed. This can mean being direct with an organizer: 'I want a different lectern.' 'Is any other kind of chair available?' 'Can I do this without a microphone?' Very often, asking for help successfully is about knowing what you want and not being afraid to tell other people what that is.

223

● For many years I was pathologically incapable of saying, 'I would like more time in which to do this,' or 'If I am going to do this, I will need more money,' or 'I only want to do this if there is something else in it for me. Here's what it is.' Straightforwardness very rarely backfires.

● Who and when to ask are as important as how to ask. Take the time to figure out exactly what you want and the fastest way to a 'yes'. This will mean doing your research about the likelihood of the outcome. Are you sure that you have asked the right person and that they have a budget for that? Are you asking them at the right time of year? Are you the best person to make this request or would it be better coming from someone else?

● Other people – especially people who are senior to you and may be very busy – are not mind-readers and they cannot guess that you want more money, more responsibility, more freedom, a four-day week, more admin support. Formulate what you need and ask for it. If they say no, ask what would have to change for them to say yes. (Try to do this in a non-passive-aggressive way. This might take practice, if you're like me.)

LIFT

● Be kind to others when they ask for help. It takes a lot to humble yourself and reach out to someone else.

● As someone once said to me: 'The next best thing to a yes is a swift no.' If you know you can't help, say so and be straightforward about it. If you have another idea of how this person could get what they want, say so. Don't say, 'I'll think about how we can make this happen,' unless you are really going to think about it and make it happen. (This is mostly a note to myself, as I say this all the time and then do nothing.) When we say things like this, we are trying to sugarcoat the no, and this is cruel. Sometimes a no is a no. Do the other person the courtesy of treating them like an adult and assume they'll be able to handle it.

● If you know you are in a position to give help and it's easy for you and costs you nothing, think about offering it. Sometimes there are things we can do to help that are really easy for us but mean a big deal to other people. (It can sometimes be hard to work out what those things are because they're so easy for us we don't realize their worth.) As soon as you realize that you are able to do something for others that matches this description, offer it far and wide. Others may be too nervous to ask. Let them know it's there.

● Be gracious about people refusing your help. Sometimes, circumstances change. Sometimes, there is other stuff going on that we can know nothing about. Just think that you will be saving up good karma for the future. Take a deep breath and light a meditation candle. (I am only partly joking.)

● You are not obliged to respond to inappropriate requests for help, especially when the help you are being asked to give is not within your gift. Sometimes, we all have to learn that an absence of a response is (a) no without having to say no and (b) an indication that you asked the wrong person or you asked at the wrong time or you should not have asked at all. An email nudge to pull a missed email to the top of someone's inbox is acceptable, after a few days or a week. But take the hint if that too is ignored.

11

How to Recruit Allies
(Hello, Men)

> '*I have yet to hear a man ask for advice on how to combine marriage and a career.*'
>
> Gloria Steinem

Is it patronizing to suggest women need help? Some men — and women - think so. Which is why there is resistance in some quarters towards opening up this discussion about what can be done to level the playing field. At a recent event, I was talking about women, public speaking and confidence, and how these things affect progress. It was a City event, heavily male in attendance, mildly hostile. The hostility was to be expected and I don't mind it: people are quite rightly sceptical if a premise is introduced that even vaguely suggests that men and women are different and merit different treatment. I was suggesting that the context for women at work is different: they experience challenges in speaking up and in feeling heard. People want to know exactly what you mean by this and where you stand. Are you a man-hater? Are you a special pleader? Or do you, as the speaker, understand that it's nuanced? By the end I could tell that people got what I was talking about and most of the questions were about what could be done to encourage women and support them without being patronizing. Which is helpful.

However. At the end, a man stood up to berate me. At the time, Theresa May was prime minister of the UK, as he reminded everyone. And women were in charge in government in both Belfast and Edinburgh. So what was I complaining about? There were clearly no barriers to women, he argued, if these particular women could make it through. We've all heard this one before. I remember a radio interview where a male writer was up against a woman in a debate and the woman was arguing about gender discrimination and he said something like, 'Well, you've managed to make it on to the radio. What are you complaining about?' As if one woman's achievement represents the achievement of all women. The argument goes something like this: 'If one woman has managed to escape the kitchen (or the garden shed or the sex dungeon), then the rest of you have no excuse.' To be honest, once someone heads off along these lines, it's pointless trying to convert them because they are clearly an idiot.

In some ways, though, I have a tiny ounce of sympathy for this foolish point of view. Because we as women can be deeply hypocritical about these things. We want equality, the same opportunities, the same money. We want to be appreciated for who we are as individuals. But at the same time we all want to claim the success of Beyoncé or Michelle Obama or Oprah Winfrey as 'belonging' to us: 'You go, girl! Women are amazing! Women are so inspiring!' This is completely understandable and laudable. We all do it and we should continue to do it. Because we need these role models and we need inspiration in a world where the chips are still stacked against us. But we also need to be cautious of this and aware of what it can look like. Because it's a reverse image of the patriarchy. Previously, men were silently, invisibly and unconsciously celebrated for being men: electing, choosing and championing men makes sense in a world biased towards men. We don't want to simply reverse this. Whatever change we push for needs to be meaningful. It needs to be as permanent as possible and it needs to represent true equality. Not just: 'You've been chosen because you're an amazing woman!' This man's question irritated me. And I wished he hadn't felt the need to ask it. Not least because he had just made every woman in the room hate him. But I was also glad of it. We need the reminder that there are some contradictions here. And, no, we do not want to be given special sweeties and a hutch for fluffy bunny rabbits in the corner office just because we are women and we're going to be bringing 'a woman's touch'. And, yes, if Theresa May can, if Margaret Thatcher can . . . We get it. But please don't tell us things are fine as they are. Because we can all see that they're not.

We will keep needing to suck up a ton of necessary evils on the way to meeting these challenges and making both society and the workplace truly more equal – and not just equal for the few (usually white, usually middle-class, usually lavishly educated) women who make it to the top. Most people feel uncomfortable around affirmative action, diversity hiring, positive discrimination and quotas. It makes sense that we feel uncomfortable as these ideas offend our natural sense of fairness. But we need to get over that discomfort and acknowledge that although the solutions may not be ideal, at least they address some of the unfairness. The situation that we have is imperfect. It will require imperfect solutions and some mistakes to fix it. At some point we might also need to let go of the idea that 'women are amazing' because there is never going to be any true equality until an incompetent, stupid and awful woman is able to rise to the same level as an incompetent, stupid and awful man. I am so ready for this role. I have been training my whole life. Please pick me. Let me be the incompetent woman. I am ready. Or probably I'm not and that's what makes me a bit incompetent. Crack on.

What is an 'ally'?

In my mind I have formed a fantasy version of Colin Firth as a person who represents a good 'ally' in a world where it is difficult to be an 'ally' without coming across as patronizing, try-hard or a bit creepy. (To be fair, my fantasy version of Colin Firth is very close to the real version of Colin Firth.) For anyone who is thinking, 'What is an ally? Why are you talking about the Second World War?', a quick side note: an ally is a man who supports women in the fight for equality. This sounds like a no-brainer, but it's painfully complicated. It's easy to be a bit wary around self-appointed 'brothers' who want to shout in your face that they are a 'male feminist' and very earnestly ask what they can do to advance the cause of their 'sisters'. However, this response is very cynical and hypocritical, as no gains are going to be made without men being on board. And we as women are constantly asking for help and trying to broaden this issue out so that women's networking events are not just full of women complimenting each other on their shoes and complaining about everything. So we have to find a way forward with the idea of the ally, without making men feel like patriarchy is entirely their fault and without making them think that they will be crushed underfoot by the weight of supernaturally empowered female anger.

Please support me in the idea that Firth is a good

candidate for a model ally. He is one of several actors who have walked away from projects associated with people caught up in #MeToo allegations and he went on the record to express his regret that he didn't personally advocate on behalf of a colleague who had complained to him about Harvey Weinstein. We are in the infancy of being able to talk about these things and figure out what we expect from men in terms of support, whether it's words or action. Do we expect men to leap on to their desks at work and shout, 'I denounce Harvey Weinstein!' so that we know where they stand? Or is it enough for them to look at the floor in embarrassment whenever anyone discusses equal pay, whilst mumbling, 'To be honest, I am not paid that much myself anyway'? Just as it's hard sometimes for women to know how to assert themselves, it's hard for men to know how to offer support and solidarity.

Women can be sceptical about the sincerity of male declarations of deeply held feminism. Men are sometimes afraid to speak up or express support because they could come across as pandering or obsequious. Or because they are afraid of saying the wrong thing. Some men say that they are feminists in order to get laid. And some men are genuinely concerned about equality in society, not just in support of women that they know but because it just feels right. Without these conversations being open and fluid, a 'them' and 'us' situation can very easily open up. I recently had an interesting conversation with a man who worked in a union and had made it his business for a long time to ensure that women in his industry received equal pay. He prided himself on his ability to champion women without seeming condescending. Then, in a meeting, someone referred to him as an 'ally'. It made him feel really uncomfortable. 'I never thought of myself as separate from my female colleagues,' he said. He went very quiet. 'I thought it was a "one of us" thing. And this made me feel like I was "one of them".' He didn't think that he was separate from the female colleagues he was fighting for. He thought he was part of the same group. He didn't want to see himself as a sympathetic outsider. He didn't want to be an 'ally' in someone's else's fight. He considered himself part of the fight.

This is a major theme emerging in many sectors, often behind closed doors, because no one wants to talk publicly about what they're doing for women's equality in case they strike the wrong note. What can men do? Should they just keep out of it? Women's groups in corporates are facing a dilemma: if they want men's help, how do they encourage men to be a part of the discussion, whilst still being supportive to women and sometimes holding women-only events? Should they avoid women-only events because they exclude men? At a big event for women I attended recently, one of the slight missteps was a panel of three middle-aged white male self-identifying 'allies' who all talked about how they try to help women. It was well meant, but it didn't quite work. It felt like another way of giving men the spotlight whilst at the same time making it look as if women 'blame' them and they, the men, were there to jolly well account for themselves. None of those impressions are helpful. But because it's hard to talk about, we avoid talking about it and the cycle persists.

There are a lot of 'necessary evils' to accept here. Perhaps it was better to have that panel than not have it, even if it felt as if it didn't quite fit with the tone of the event. Perhaps that panel needed to happen in order for people to see that an all-male panel at an all-female event looks odd. We need to open up these conversations and be prepared for them to be awkward.

Can you call someone an 'ally'?

I actually have some hesitation about using the word 'ally'. Not everyone is comfortable using it. Your familiarity and comfort around this word will depend a lot on your age and very probably on how much you use social media. I hear it used increasingly in the corporate world, where people are starting to understand exactly what it means. But it is something of an exclusive word that suggests, rather unhelpfully, that you have to be an ally to know what an ally is.

The word 'ally' first began to be used in a non-military

context in connection with the LGBT movement in the 1970s. Back then, if you were straight but you supported LGBT rights, you were called an ally. The concept has since been borrowed by feminism (i.e. you're a man but you support the advancement of women). It's also used around issues of race, minority, diversity and intersectionality (for example, if you're white but you know about 'checking your privilege' i.e. admitting that you benefit from the status quo), around transgender issues if you are cisgender (i.e. your gender identity matches the gender you were assigned at birth but you make an attempt to understand the concerns of trans people) and around disability issues (i.e. you are able-bodied but you advocate alongside those who are not). Clearly, it's morally right to be an 'ally' to others. To say you are not an ally is in effect to declare that you are an enemy. But, for some, the language itself can feel distancing.

There is a mass of discomfort around all these issues because it can be difficult to talk about, especially in a work context where everyone is so scared of getting something wrong. Some people might feel it's important to ask others if they are allies and that we have to encourage people to check their privilege. In principle, those people are right, of course. In reality, they have not had to go into a board meeting in a room where everyone on that board has looked a particular way since time immemorial and feels very threatened by the idea of change.

LIFT AS YOU CLIMB

In the financial sector I have had senior men at several companies boast to me with great pride that they have a woman (a woman!) in place at the highest levels in their company, and I know they are talking about a woman who is in a position where she is the only one amongst over twenty or thirty men. In this context, you are supposed to be impressed that they have any women at all because for many hundreds of years they had none. In some industries, this is what we are up against and this is what we have to face: slow progress, constant jockeying for position, backlash. This is the business of one step forward, two steps back, and the ongoing arguments about tokenism, 'virtue-signalling' and 'diversity hires'.

From all the conversations I have had on the subject of inclusion, I surmise that no one has found the right answer to getting men involved in pushing for equality and some people positively squirm even to think about it. In general, the younger the average age of the workforce, the easier it is to talk about these things. Perhaps if older people near the top of a company realized how embarrassingly antiquated they look to younger people further down the company, they would change pretty quickly. Many senior people are just not aware of this conversation and how younger people take it for granted. And a lot of younger people don't really know just how dismissive older people can be about it when they're not talking publicly.

238

It's a tricky situation that is only going to be resolved through experimentation. Finding out what is working for others is always useful. So ask people outside your own workplace, 'What does your company do about this? What has worked? What has been a disaster? What language do you use?' If you want to get men involved, find a man whom everyone generally likes and who has a reputation as easygoing, someone who is as senior as possible but also as approachable as possible. Get him on board and explain to him that there is already a women's group or there is going to be a women's group and would he like to be involved? This works best where it happens in a relaxed and informal way and where you try your best (although this is very difficult) not to mention the men in the room and point out that they're in the minority for once, et cetera. (No judgement. We've all done it.) If you run a women's network, you need to schedule events that are not only attractive to women: men also want to learn how to network, how to be better speakers, how to have a better work–life balance, how to negotiate for more money. People will say to me: 'We have a women's networking group and we really want men to come, but they never do.' And I ask, 'What was your last event?' And the answer is, 'Oh, it was a handbag designer talking about her career.' There's your answer right there.

239

What if people are openly hostile? Or they pretend to be 'allies' but do nothing?

Not everyone recognizes that equality is important. Some people are threatened by it. Some people think it's patronizing (because 'everyone must be allowed to rise on merit' and they don't recognize their own privilege). Some think it has been tried and has failed. Others think feminism has 'gone too far'. Or that quotas are a disaster because everyone will assume that you can't do your job; you've only been put there because your face fits.

You have to pick your battles. Some people are not going to be converted to this cause and you may have to work alongside them anyway. If you find yourself in this kind of environment, then you have to resort to resilience training. Keep your morale up, monitor your mental health, keep an eye on your stress management and make sure your motivation is boosted. If your spirits slide, it becomes very difficult to have a sense of humour about inequality and to have any sympathy for anyone who has a different point of view to you. Sometimes that feeling can be a sign that you're not working in the right place. So go and find a job where there are 'allies' instead of 'enemies'. But sometimes we need to stay where we are in order to progress or because we love our work. We don't want to be forced out because of one person's closed attitudes or because the company ethos is evolving too slowly.

Managing your morale is the most important factor influencing the success of your working life. Whether you can keep your spirits up. It sounds basic, but in any walk of life most of us are focused on advancement, time management, financials and working out who is in our corner and who is not. In reality, none of this matters unless your own state of mind is in a good place. Managing your morale as a freelancer, for example, means not overworking, making sure you spend time with other people instead of being alone too much, finding ways to be resilient about rejection and being optimistic but realistic about your finances. In the workplace, managing your morale is a different but related project. It might mean not getting caught up in toxic working practices that everyone else treats as normal (coming in early and working late, for example). It might mean finding friends and colleagues outside of your department so that you are not too isolated. It might mean organizing social activities with your colleagues so that you get to know their non-work selves. Or it could mean the opposite – avoiding work social activities because everyone has got into the habit of being in a drunken mess at these events and moaning about everything. It might mean avoiding certain colleagues who make 'jokes' that are borderline sexist. Or setting a deadline: if they're still bugging you to death in six months' time, you'll report them. Managing your morale really means knowing what's good for you and making yourself stick to it.

CLIMB

Disclaimer: the following tips are all intended for men (or 'allies') wanting to help lift women. I'm not including any tips to help men climb because, let's face it, they don't need any help in that department.

LIFT

● Well-meaning gentlemen! Please do not put in your Twitter profile (or similar) that you are a feminist. It's like saying in your profile that you are not a racist. In essence: we should hope so! Feminist is not something that a person is. Feminism is something that must be done, sometimes invisibly. It is an active pursuit. It is not a passive state of being.

● There are some really practical things men can do - and these are also useful for women, especially if you are thinking about encouraging younger colleagues, promoting inclusion of all kinds and generally making sure that the world is not replicated in our own images. If you are asked to appear on a panel, say you'd like to check that it's a diverse selection of people. I've also said on occasion: 'I don't really want to be on a panel where everyone looks and sounds like me. Can you reassure me that won't be the case?' If every man who is ever asked to do an event said this, things would be fixed very quickly.

243

• If you've got a lot on or you know that you don't need an opportunity, recommend a female colleague. Think about inclusion when you're saying no. We all need to make it easier to find people.

• Advocate for people (of all kinds) who are not the alphas in a room. If you find yourself in a situation where you are one of many men in a room with few women, be aware of the dynamics. Who is speaking the most and the loudest? Who needs help speaking up? (This won't always be a woman. If I am in the room, I will not require any help speaking up.)

• No one wants to censor anyone's humour (within reason) or impose a worldwide ban on the *Carry On* film franchise. I hate the idea of people policing their language and their banter. However, it's worth thinking about context and who's in the room. What would be funny and irreverent and maverick with friends or people who know you well can be too much around people at work who don't know you very well or who see life differently from you. Similarly, making jokes about how it is no longer OK to make jokes any more is tricky. This makes it sound as if you would really like to make a rape joke but you're being really generous in holding yourself back. (Thanks for not telling us your rape joke. We really appreciate your restraint.) If you do hear someone else making a joke or a throwaway comment and you can feel other people flinch, be the one who says something. I will always say something like, 'I am not going to take offence at that because I am a free-and-easy kind of lady. But, seriously, is that really necessary?' or 'I am going to ignore the fact that you said that as you probably already want to take it back,' or even 'There's no way I would report a comment like that because I am not that kind of person. But someone else easily could.' Everyone knows that this is all code for: 'Don't be a dick.'

CONCLUSION

The Business of Finding Your Own Path Through All This (and Making Peace with Not Being the Perfect Sister)

When it comes to thinking about sisterhood and where we stand as individuals on the responsibility to support other women, I am quite literally a terrible sister. My own sister is three years younger than me and I was pretty mean to her as a child. On one occasion I hid under her bed and then jumped out in order to frighten her. She was so angry that she bit me square on the nose. I was about six years old at the time. But I'm not sure this excuses me from what was essentially psychopathic behaviour. Somehow my sister and I got past it, though. And she only reminds me about it every other time I see her. We all make mistakes in regard to our sisters (both our sisters by birth and our sisters in womanhood) and we need to forgive ourselves for not being perfect.

The fact is that we don't really know what sisterly support looks like in the adult world until we start labelling it and defining it. It's common for women to moan about their female bosses - the 'nightmare women' who have managed them - or to bitch about female colleagues. And it is absolutely human nature to be irritated by annoying people (whether men or women). It is sometimes healthy to vent and complain. But if you only notice the people who are holding you back and spend a lot of time examining exactly how frustrating and stupid and callous they are, then you have less time left over for analysing the behaviour of the people who are quietly supporting and helping you. We often ask each other, for example, how we can survive a mean or difficult colleague. We rarely pinpoint our unofficial mentors, the tacit cheerleaders and the unsung heroines of our daily lives.

There are two good reasons to spend time thinking about what constitutes your own definition of support, whether it's the support you expect from others or the support you hope to offer. The first is that it's better for our mental health if we are focused on the positive. If there are serious negatives in our lives at work – unequal pay, bullying, name-calling – we need to find ways to address those things. But low-level annoyances about what's holding us back at different times in our working lives can become all-consuming and draining. The energy we spend kvetching about these things can be better spent cultivating the strengths of people around us. Instead of looking at who to blame, who can we thank? Instead of having a moan session with a friend after work ('Here are ninety-seven reasons why I hate Janice in IT'), have a praise session ('My colleague Janice did this amazing thing for me today').

The second reason to consider what support means

to you is that by naming these positives and articulating them, we become more aware of them and able to attract more of this behaviour by encouraging it in others. We all do good things that go unnoticed. How great would it be if all the good things we did became noticed and were highlighted?

There's no need to think of yourself as some kind of martyr or angel or saint by putting these ideas to the front of your mind. It's much better to support other women and encourage this concept of lifting imperfectly, occasionally and clumsily than it is not to do it at all. This is why the idea of 'a special place in hell' has always bothered me. It feels like such a gigantic responsibility and such a huge failure if you don't live up to what other women might expect of you. It makes you feel like giving up before you've even started, as though there is some kind of mythical Judge of Sisterhood who is going to descend from the skies and say in a booming voice: 'You have failed other women.' Once you've had that vision of the Judge of Sisterhood you tend towards thinking, 'Who am I to help anyone else? I'm barely managing myself.'

Many of us spend too much energy worrying about all the ways we're failing ourselves and failing others. Are we too ambitious or not ambitious enough? Have we done enough to help other women or is it too much of an ask when life is already a pain? We need to take a deep breath, let go of a lot of these fixed expectations

251

and be open to moving forward with an attitude of curiosity. What might this lifting look like in your world? What are the limits of climbing for you? Who can you start a conversation with about this? There is no road map for this behaviour as women have only been in leadership positions in the workplace and in charge of their own destinies for the past few decades. All this is new. And whilst this idea of lifting as you climb might be culturally powerful and we might feel that it's important and right, we don't spend enough time defining what it actually looks and feels like.

There is no one way either to lift or to climb. For different women, these things will have completely opposing definitions, and that's OK. In family life the relationships between sisters look very different. Some sisters get on by competing (gently) with each other. Some copy each other's behaviour. Some sisters show their love to each other by taking turns to be the 'strong' one. Sisterhood in society and the workplace can be similarly beautifully complicated. Sometimes lifting another woman means being cruel to be kind. We have all had moments when we have had to find the honesty to tell a friend that her behaviour is not helping her or when we have had to have a quiet word with a colleague. Equally, sometimes climbing means focusing on yourself for a while and recognizing that you are not able to be as generous with others as you'd like. The whole idea is about flexibility, experimentation and openness, rather than some kind of edict that you must be ambitious at all times and simultaneously help other women. Because trying to do everything at once and trying to do the best for yourself whilst looking after everyone else and never messing up and being consistently flawless is completely impossible.

It's also not about never criticizing other women or giving all behaviour a free pass just because someone is a woman and she's your sister and so you can never tell her she's wrong. (My own sister will be very glad to read this and I expect a phone call any minute now.) Part of the business of equality is about holding each other to account, being able to criticize each other and being able to be objective. We do not do anything for other women in the long term if we promote and champion others purely on the grounds that they are women. No one wants to hear that they are a diversity hire, even if diversity hiring is something that needs to happen. We need to find a way to be balanced and subtle about this. We need to try to be fair, to create opportunities for others, to recognize that the playing field is not level and that something needs to be done to address this. But also to recognize that there are no perfect answers, that we are all stumbling our way through life and that we all have bad days when we revert to our less noble, childish selves and might well be tempted to hide under someone's bed in order to annoy them. (Please don't do this: you will get teeth marks on your nose.)

LIFT AS YOU CLIMB

The idea of lifting as you climb has to be fun, enriching and invigorating. It can't be just another exhausting duty for the to-do list. Quite frankly, women already have so many things that they feel they 'must' and 'should' do that I couldn't bear the thought of anyone thinking, 'Oh, great. I'm doing all this stuff already and now I have to help other women up the ladder too? Thanks, but no thanks.' The antidote to this attitude – and we all have those moments – is to force yourself to be reminded of all the women whose shoulders you stand on, all the women who have ever done anything to make your life easier and all the women who are waiting to help you, if only you reach out. There is more support outside of us than we think. And there is more support inside of us waiting to be gifted to others than we ever imagined. Go and climb and lift and climb. And then lift and climb some more. It's OK if you slip. One of us will be there to push you back up.

'I do my best because I'm counting on you counting on me.'
Maya Angelou

FURTHER READING

Here are some books I have found useful recently and over the years in understanding my thinking around the topic of women and ambition – and also in changing myself.

- Leslie Bennetts, *The Feminine Mistake: Are We Giving Up Too Much?* (Voice, 2007). This is a fantastic read on money, economics and power. Bennetts looks at the 'double bind' that many women face: they feel that they need to be both a primary parent and a breadwinner. This is almost an impossibility and forces many women either to give up earning (and raise their family instead) or to give up on the idea that they can have a family whilst still working.

- Brené Brown, *Dare to Lead: Brave Work, Tough Conversations, Whole Hearts* (Vermilion, 2018). This builds on the ideas in Brown's other books, *Daring Greatly* and *Rising Strong*, and brings her work on vulnerability and shame into the world of leadership and work. What I like most about her message is that it's about experimentation: we have to learn to take risks in order to do things differently.

- Caroline Criado Perez, *Invisible Women: Exploring Data Bias in a World Designed for Men* (Chatto and Windus, 2019). If you want chapter and verse on the context for discrimination against women, plus loads of statistics and scientific evidence that will get you riled up . . . this is the book to do it.

- Meghan Daum, *The Problem with Everything: My Journey through the New Culture Wars* (Gallery Books, 2019). Tired of meaningless labels like 'snowflake' and 'woke', Daum explores why we are so conflicted on the subject of feminism, gender and identity politics, and asks how we can rediscover the centre ground.

- Jinny Ditzler, *Your Best Year Yet! The Ten Questions That Will Change Your Life For Ever* (Harper Element, 2006). This is very self-helpy, but if you are at a point where you are completely lost and need some guidance on what to do next, this book asks the right questions. One of the hardest parts of ambition is knowing what you want and what your priorities are and this book has some great exercises for pinning that down.

- Lori Gottlieb, *Maybe You Should Talk to Someone: Life from Both Sides of the Couch* (Scribe UK, 2019). A fantastic memoir about a therapist who finds herself at a point of crisis after a break-up and has to work out how therapy can help her, when she thought she knew it all. Along the way she reveals why it's so important to understand our own internal workings and anxieties and how much we all have in common in terms of the stresses that obsess us. Also funny.

- Spencer Johnson, *Who Moved My Cheese: An Amazing Way to Deal with Change in Your Work and in Your Life* (Vermilion, 2002). This is an old-school self-help classic: a parable of some mice who live in a maze and wake up one day to find that all the delicious cheese they loved to eat has suddenly disappeared. Where can they find new cheese? For 'cheese', read 'inspiration' or 'ambition'. A very useful quick shot in the arm, and also a reminder not to take the subject of life strategy too seriously.

- Michelle Obama, *Becoming* (Viking, 2018). An obvious example for inspiration and motivation, but a useful one because this book is beautifully written, never talks down to the reader and illustrates what ambition looks like when it's balanced: where personal life matters just as much as work.

- Mary Portas, *Work Like a Woman: A Manifesto for Change* (Bantam Press, 2018). This is a practical and inspiring read on how to get ahead in the workplace without compromising your personal values. Portas writes from experience and her views feel like part of a new movement to bring kindness, compassion, altruism and long-term thinking into the world of work. We don't quite know what this new world is going to look like yet, but this is a great place to start.

- Anne-Marie Slaughter, *Unfinished Business: Women Men Work Family* (Oneworld Publications, 2016). Foreign policy analyst and academic Slaughter served as Director of Policy Planning for the US State Department under Secretary of State Hillary Clinton. This book arose from an article she wrote ('Why Women Still Can't Have It All') about trying to do that job whilst raising two teenage boys.

Two books I mention constantly, as they have made a huge difference to my life, are *Playing Big: A Practical Guide for Brilliant Women Like You* by Tara Mohr (Arrow, 2015) and *Better Than Before: Mastering the Habits of Our Everyday Lives* by Gretchen Rubin (Thorndike, 2015). Both these authors also have an array of resources online available for free. Tara Mohr's work is about uncovering the internal barriers that are holding you back. How is your 'inner critic' talking to you and how can you turn down that voice? In what ways are you 'hiding' in your work and in your life? What would represent a 'leap' for you that would suddenly drive everything forward?

Gretchen Rubin has devoted her life to understanding what makes us more productive. Why do some people find it harder than others to maintain good habits? How do you become more self-disciplined? How can you make change easier by working with your own inclinations rather than against them?

ACKNOWLEDGEMENTS

I have to acknowledge a debt to many women (and men) in the creation of this book, which is the result of a lot of thinking, awkward conversations and experiments on myself over many years. But most of all I owe a debt to readers. This book is the result of a lot of face-to-face and social media interactions over the past two years. Without the honesty and openness of these interactions, I would not have understood how important it is to open up a conversation about ambition and what we understand by it. So to everyone who supported the book and the podcast *How to Own the Room: Women and the Art of Brilliant Speaking*: thank you. This book would not exist without your feedback.

A lot of the ideas in this book arose from reactions to *How to Own the Room*, especially at live events and in workshops. Women's thoughts on public speaking, power and taking up space made me realize that a lot of the issues in this area are connected to our feelings of discomfort and confusion about ambition. Thank you in particular to John Gordon and all the team at How To Academy, who saw the potential for 'live' encounters around this topic before anyone else did.

I owe so much to all the team at Transworld, who

really live this idea of 'altruistic ambition' every day in the way they work. Thank you to Andrea Henry for her sensitive and patient editing and to Kate Samano and Alex Newby for their beady eyes. Thanks to Alison Barrow, always full of ideas and enthusiasm. To Jo Thomson for her fantastic design work. And to everyone who contributed inspiration and sweat: Antonia Whitton, Alice Murphy-Pyle, Ella Horne and Helena Gonda at The Flip. The ideas and spirit of Sophie Christopher were infused in this project from the beginning. I bow to Cathryn Summerhayes, who lifts many whilst climbing like a demon mountaineer.

I have personally benefited from the actions – intentional and unintentional – of women who lift as they climb without even thinking about it. In journalism I was lucky enough to come under the unofficial mentorship of Rosie Boycott, Sue Matthias, Kath Viner, Kira Cochrane, Katherine Butler, Sam Baker and Veronica Wadley. Thanks to Isabel Berwick and Emma Jacobs at the *Financial Times* for recent lifting and to all the team at FT Comment. Many friends and colleagues in comedy and writing have influenced the thinking in this book, and I'm particularly indebted to the support of Lucy Porter, Jessica Fostekew, Maggie Tibble, Jane Lindsey, Margaret Heffernan, Maura Wilding, Uzma Hameed, Julia Hornsby and Sarah Hurwitz.

The biggest thank-you goes to the people who get pushed to the back of the queue occasionally (only occasionally) while all this lifting and climbing is going on: my husband Simon and my children Will, Vera and Jack. And to the person who supports all of us: Ola Majerz. This book is dedicated to my sister, Trudy Groskop, who always reminds me what really matters. Finally, I need to apologize to anyone who is reading this and thinking, 'Well, Viv has certainly never lifted me as she climbs.' So to everyone whose email I forgot to reply to, who I brushed past at a party because I was desperate for the loo, or who I promised to send that thing to and then the thing never arrived . . . I'm sorry. I owe you a drink.

Viv Groskop is a writer, stand-up comedian and TV and radio presenter. She has hosted book tours for Graham Norton and Jo Brand, is the veteran of four Edinburgh Fringe shows and fronts the Top 10 iTunes podcast *How to Own the Room*. She has presented BBC Radio 4's *Front Row* and *Saturday Review* and appears regularly on BBC2's *Newsnight*. As an executive coach, she works with women – and occasionally men – across business, media and advertising, helping them to hone their authority, presence and leadership.